Where Is Your
Body?

MARI J. MATSUDA

Where Is Your
Body?

AND

OTHER

ESSAYS ON

RACE

GENDER

AND THE

LAW

BEACON PRESS

Boston

Beacon Press
25 Beacon Street
Boston, Massachusetts 02108-2892

Beacon Press books
are published under the auspices of the
Unitarian Universalist Association of Congregations.

© 1996 by Mari J. Matsuda

Text design: Lucinda L. Hitchcock

LIBRARY OF CONGRESS CATALOGING-IN-PUBLICATION DATA
Matsuda, Mari J., 1956–
    Where is your body? : and other essays on race, gender, and the law / Mari
Matsuda.
        p.   cm.
    Includes index.
    ISBN 0-8070-6780-6 (cloth)
    1. Group identity—Political aspects—United States. 2. Social
change—United States. 3. Equality—United States. 4. Feminism—
United States. 5. Minorities—United States—Political activity. 6. Political
correctness—United States. 7. Education, Higher—Political aspects—
United States. 8. United States—Social policy—1993-   I. Title
    E184.A1M314   1996
    305'.0973—dc20   96-25498

To Charles Radford Lawrence III

freedom fighter and father of three angels

Contents

Introduction

It is a contradiction of our times that the gatekeepers of knowledge can enhance their position by welcoming an occasional visit from the traveling diva. That is a term bell hooks once used for outspoken women of color who challenge orthodoxy in the academy. As grand divas like bell hooks, Patricia Williams, and Catharine MacKinnon have found, places like Harvard and Yale want a diva visit but not a diva invasion. Come for tea, but please do not expect to stay.

There are few Asian-American women in the academy, particularly in law. When I started, I was the only one, walking into an empty space marked "Asian women." This vacuum made me a traveling diva by default. If they needed one, I was it. Thus the many calls and invitations that planted the seeds of this book.

Several years ago, an Asian-American student called to ask for a reading list and to complain about her womens studies professor. The student had gone to her professor to ask why there were no Asian women writers on the syllabus. Her professor answered, "This is a theory course. There aren't any Asian women doing theory."

On the one hand, I had some empathy for the professor because I have often been on the receiving end of student complaints that their particular perspective was left out of a syllabus crammed full of retrievals of the absent. They do not complain to their contracts professor, but they complain to me because of the implicit promise in my courses that we will leave no one behind in our work to uncover and struggle against subordination.

I also fear they complain to me for another reason: the cultural code that tells them that someone who looks like me is supposed to take care of their feelings.

While I identified with the woman professor subject to complaints about her syllabus, I shared the outrage of the student who called me for help and remain haunted by the words, "There are no Asian women doing theory."

I know of Asian women running battered women's shelters, figuring out how many different kinds of rice to keep in stock to make sure that women of different Asian ethnicities feel at home in the kitchen; figuring out why the kitchen is important; and figuring out how patriarchy defines masculinity and then takes it away, as defined, from Asian men, creating flashpoints that end up scarring women's bodies. This is theory.

I read Asian women writers. I read their anthologies, their novels, and their self-consciously postmodern papers presented at academic conferences. This is theory.

I call the words in this book theory, in the face of a world that still believes, still knows with casual certainty, that I do not exist. A female Asian-American radical law professor who does theory is not something most people have come in contact with, and therefore it is a null set to them.

The works collected here are, for the most part, lectures and speeches I was invited to make at places where there were no Asian women on the faculty, or in venues where Asian women had not spoken before. What you will read is a speaking voice, not a high-theory voice, attempting to share ideas and politics with rooms full of mostly strangers. At least some in my audiences learned that there are Asian women legal theorists, but it is also true that coming for a day did little to change the deep structures of institutions that have for centuries erased the presence, the thought, and the action of women of color.

I am grateful for and acknowledge those many folks who so graciously invited me to speak or write in particular fora. Some invitations came from activist community groups who needed speakers for fund-raisers and small, local events. Speaking at such functions is speaking at home, and the language of those essays is a home language, directed intimately at a particular audience while inviting others to listen in. At other times, my hosts were students or marginalized faculty who waged internal battles to bring someone like me to their campus, to speak in the language of the academy. Sometimes true liberals at the top levels—deans and administrators who believe in and practice the tradition of welcoming competing thought—initiated the visit.

In each case, I spoke from my position as a sansei feminist committed to ending all forms of subordination. The first theme embedded in these essays is thus identity. Who I am in relation to the historical forces that constrain my choices and options is critical to my understanding of law and justice. This is not the same as saying, in a determinist or simplistic way, that identity is fixed, that it is everything, or that it is an end in itself. Rather, I look to my own experience and the experience of others like me to understand the world and to decide how to move it. I believe in individual responsibility and human agency. All of us can work for a more just world. Nothing about who we are prevents that. *Where Is Your Body?* asks how it is that where we stand shapes what we see, what we believe, and what privileges and subordinations we experience.

It is currently fashionable in theoretical circles to attack essentialism—the view that identity necessarily means a fixed experience and outlook. There is a regressive and a progressive

version of this critique. Regressive anti-essentialism says, "All
women are not alike; therefore it is pointless to seek the inclusion and representation of women through programs like affirmative action." This is exactly what federal courts are doing with
the theory of anti-essentialism. The Fifth Circuit Court of Appeals, in its opinion attacking affirmative action, said that seeking a racially diverse student body at the University of Texas Law
School presumed that all members of a minority racial group
shared a diverse perspective.[1] Because this was a false assumption, the court said, racial diversity was not a legitimate goal. In
this version of anti-essentialism, the history of vicious discrimination in public education in Texas is ignored, and the school is
allowed to revert to what it was for years: all white.

Progressive anti-essentialism is quite a different animal. Recognizing that not all people in a given category think alike is occasion for more diversity, not less. In my own community, for
example, there is more political division than in most ethnic
groups. To represent the full spectrum of Asian-American experience in a given institution requires more than a token presence. One traveling diva once a year will not do it, nor will hiring
one as a permanent fixture. At every law school I have taught at,
I was the only Asian woman, and I was faced with the impossi-
bility of representing all Asian women with my lone presence.

A second theme, related to identity, is the power of language.
Claiming identity is a manipulation of the ideal world: a use of
language to construct a new space in people's brains. Saying I am
Asian and feminist and radical and a law professor and a product
of affirmative action challenges existing assumptions that Asian
women are compliant, good with numbers and not words, sexually available, and not in need of affirmative action. It also chal-

lenges the view that benefiting from affirmative action is something shameful rather than a source of pride in the door-opening struggles of the past.

Language can construct understanding, language can assault, and language can exclude. Words have power. Theory is not the key to social change, and words alone cannot end subordination, but words are part of the struggle. In addressing the PC debate, academic freedom, sexual harassment, and assaultive speech, this book recognizes language as an important battleground.

Finally, my position is explicitly left and political. My teachers are those engaged in struggle, those who work to understand their own position in structures of domination and oppression, and those who act to dismantle those structures. My own parents, lifelong members of the peace, labor, and civil rights movements, taught me the politics and ethics that guide this book. Their teachings were straightforward: every human being counts, each is entitled to flourish, structures that deny that right are unstable and will end, a good life is one struggling toward that ending.

Whether addressing law, language, or theory, I am guided by those lessons and by the voices in my own generation who asked, in a challenging and uncompromising voice, Where is your body?

---

1   *Hopwood v. State of Texas,* 78 F. 3d 932 (5th Cir., 1996).

PART I

WHERE IS YOUR BODY? *Politics and Identity*

1

Multiple Consciousness as Jurisprudential Method

This chapter was presented at the Yale Law School conference on women of color and the law, April 16, 1988. That first annual Women of Color and the Law Conference was organized by a student collective. I deliberately opened this talk with an image of white women to illustrate that putting women of color at the center was an inclusive rather than exclusive effort. I had listened to conference organizers lament the struggle it took to produce the conference – the divisions among them, the resentments of white colleagues, the feelings of elation and exhaustion that accompanied their work. In thinking about the students I was invited to address, this speech wrote itself, as often happens when I identify with the audience. Written, as it was, with students in mind, this piece has become a favorite of student readers ever since it was first published by the Womens' Rights Law Reporter, *a student-run, activist journal.*

In 1868, two white women, Angelina and Sarah Grimke, acknowledged publicly that a Black man, the son of their slave-owning brother, was their nephew. They commenced to bestow on that nephew the love and familiarity due a relative. In publicly embracing their blood tie to a black man, these women were doing something unthinkable, inconceivable –

something outside the consciousness of their time. What was it that projected the thinking of these two women ahead of the thinking of their peers? It was their consciousness of oppression, a consciousness developed in their feminist and abolitionist struggles.

The confluence of the feminist and abolitionist causes marks the most progressive moments in American history. Today, the Yale Law School Women of Color Collective is claiming that progressive heritage as their own. In their honor, let us consider women of color as a paradigm group for utilization of multiple consciousness as jurisprudential method. Let us imagine a student with women-of-color consciousness sitting in class in the first year of law school. The dialogue in class is designed to force students to pare away the extraneous, to adopt the lawyer's skill of narrowing issues and delineating the scope of relevant evidence. The professor sees his job – and I use the male pronoun deliberately – as training the students out of the muddleheaded world where everything is relevant and into the lawyer's world where the few critical facts prevail.

The discussion in class today is of a *Miranda*-type case. Our student wonders whether the defendant was a person of color and whether the police officer was white. The student knows the city in which the case arose and knows that the level of police violence is so high in that place that church groups hold candlelight vigils outside the main police station every Sunday. The crime charged is rape. The student wonders about the race of the victim and whether the zealous questioning by the police in the case was tied to the victim's race. The student thinks about rape – the rape of her roommate last year and her own fears. She knows, given the prevalence of violence against women, that some of her classmates in this class of 100 students have been raped. She wonders how they are reacting to the case and what pain it resurrects for them.

In the consciousness of this student, many facts and emotions are relevant to the case that are extraneous to standard legal discourse. The student has decided to adopt standard legal discourse for the classroom and to keep her women-of-color consciousness for herself and for her support group. This bifurcated thinking is not unusual to her. She has been doing it throughout her schooling – shifting back and forth between her consciousness as a third-world person and the white consciousness required for survival in elite educational institutions.

This student, as she has become older, has learned to peel away layers of consciousness like layers of an onion. In the one class where she has a woman professor – a white woman – she feels free to raise issues of violence against women, but she decides to keep to herself another level of consciousness: her nationalist anger at white privilege and her perception that the dominant white conception of violence excludes the daily violence of ghetto poverty.

This constant shifting of consciousness produces sometimes madness, sometimes genius, and sometimes both. You can hear it in the music of Billie Holiday. You can read it in the writing of Professor Pat Williams – that shifting in and out, that tapping of a consciousness from beyond and bringing it back to the place where most people stand.

Let us give an ending to the student I described: she goes on to excel in law school, she becomes an international human rights activist and she writes poems in her kitchen while she waits for the pies to cool. She does not go mad because she

continues to meet with her support group, and they continue
to tell her, "No, you are not crazy, the world looks that way
to us, too."

What does a consciousness of the experience of life under patriarchy and racial hierarchy bring to jurisprudence? The ideas
emanating from feminist legal theorists and legal scholars of color
have important points of intersection that assist in the fundamental inquiries of jurisprudence: What is justice, and what does
law have to do with it?

Outsider scholars have recognized that their specific experiences and histories are relevant to jurisprudential inquiry. They
reject narrow evidentiary concepts of relevance and credibility.
They reject artificial bifurcation of thought and feeling. Their
anger, their pain, their daily lives, and the histories of their people are relevant to the definition of justice. "The personal is the
political," we hear from feminists, and "Everything is political,"
we hear from communities of color. Not much time is wasted
in those communities arguing over definitions of justice. Justice
means children with full bellies sleeping in warm beds under
clean sheets. Justice means no lynchings and no rapes. Justice
means access to a livelihood. It means control over one's own
body. These kinds of concrete and substantive visions of justice
flow naturally from the experience of oppression.

And what of procedure, of law? Here outsiders respond with
characteristic duality. On the one hand, they respond as legal realists, aware of the historical abuse of law to sustain existing conditions of domination. Unlike the postmodern critics of the left,
however, outsiders, including feminists and people of color,
have embraced legalism as a tool of necessity, making legal consciousness their own in order to attack injustice. Thus, to the

feminist lawyer faced with pregnant teenagers seeking abortions, it would be absurd to reject the use of an elitist legal system or the use of the concept of rights when such use is necessary to meet the immediate needs of her client. There are times to stand outside the courtroom door and say, "This procedure is a farce, the legal system is corrupt, justice will never prevail in this land as long as privilege rules in the courtroom." There are times to stand inside the courtroom and say, "This is a nation of laws, laws recognizing fundamental values of rights, equality and personhood." Sometimes, as Angela Davis did, there is a need to make both speeches in one day. Is that crazy? Inconsistent? Not to Professor Davis, a Black woman on trial for her life in racist America. It made perfect sense to her and to the twelve jurors good and true who heard her when she said, "Your government lies, but *your* law is above such lies."

Professor Davis's decision to use a dualist approach to a repressive legal system may very well have saved her life. Not only did she tap her history and consciousness as a Black, a woman, and a communist, she did so with intent and awareness. Her multiple consciousness was not a mystery to her but a well-defined and acknowledged tool of analysis, one that she was able to share with the jury.

A professor once remarked that the mediocre law students are the ones who are still trying to make it all make sense, that is, the students who are trying to understand law as necessary, logical, and coextensive with reality. The students who excel in law schools – and the best lawyers – are the ones who are able to detach law and to see it as a system that makes sense only from a particular viewpoint. Those lawyers can operate within that view and then shift out of it for purposes of critique, analysis, and strategy. The shifting of consciousness I have thus far ascribed to women of color is a tool used, in a more limited way, by skilled lawyers of many ideological bents. A good corporate lawyer can argue within the language and policy of antitrust law, modify that argument to suit a Reagan-era judge, and then advise a client that the outcome may well turn on some event in Geneva wholly irrelevant to the legal doctrine. Multiple consciousness as juris-prudential method, however, encompasses more than conscious-ness shifting as skilled advocacy. It encompasses as well the search for the pathway to a just world.

The multiple consciousness I urge lawyers to attain is not a random ability to see all points of view but a deliberate choice to see the world from the standpoint of the oppressed. That world is accessible to all of us. We should know it in its concrete par-ticulars. We should know of our sister carrying buckets of water up five flights of stairs in a welfare hotel, our sister trembling at 3 A.M. in a shelter for battered women, our sisters holding blood-ied children in their arms in Cape Town, on the West Bank, and in Nicaragua. The jurisprudence of outsiders teaches that these details and the emotions they evoke are relevant and important as we set out on the road to justice. These details are accessible to all of us, of all genders and colors. We can choose to know the lives of others by reading, studying, listening, and venturing into different places. For lawyers, our pro bono work may be the most effective means of acquiring a broader consciousness of op-pression.

Abstraction and detachment are ways out of the discomfort of direct confrontation with the ugliness of oppression. Abstrac-tion, criticized by both feminists and scholars of color, is the method that allows theorists to discuss liberty, property, and rights in the aspirational mode of liberalism with no connection to what those concepts mean in real people's lives. Much in our mainstream intellectual training values abstraction and denigrates nitty-gritty detail. Holding onto a multiple consciousness will allow us to operate both within the abstractions of standard jurisprudential discourse and within the details of our own special knowledge.

Whisperings at Yale and elsewhere about how deconstructionist heroes were closet fascists remind me of how important it is to stay close to oppressed communities. High talk about language, meaning, sign, process, and law can mask racist and sexist ugliness if we never stop to ask, "Exactly what are you talking about, and what is the implication of what your are saying for my sister who is carrying buckets of water up five flights of stairs in a welfare hotel? What do you propose to do for her *today*, not in some abstract future you are creating in your mind?" If you have been made to feel, as I have, that such inquiry is theoretically unsophisticated and quaintly naive, resist! Read what Professor Williams, Professor Scales-Trent, and other feminists and people of color are writing.[1] The reality and detail of oppression are a starting point for these writers as they enter into mainstream debates about law and theory.

For example, the ongoing dilemma of neutral principles is challenged by outsiders' reality. Legal theorists puzzle over the conflicting desire for finite and certain principles of law, free from the whims of the despot. The trouble is, then, that the law itself becomes the despot—neutral concepts of rights end up protecting corporate polluters and Ku Klux Klan hate mongers. Standard liberal thought sees no way out of this dilemma, arguing for neutrality as a first principle and the inviolability of fixed rules of law as the anchor that keeps us from drifting in a sea of varied personal preferences.

From communities of outsiders struggling around their immediate needs – for jobs, for education, for personal safety – we see new legal concepts emerging to challenge the citadel of neutrality. Proposals for nonneutral laws that will promote the human spirit include affirmative action, proposals for desegregation, proposals for curtailment of hate groups and elimination of propaganda advocating violence against women, and proposals for reparations to Native Americans for loss of their lands. All these are controversial proposals, and debates continue about their worth. The very controversy reveals how deeply they cut into the unresolved dilemma of neutrality that lies at the heart of American law. These proposals add up to a new jurisprudence, one founded not on an ideal of neutrality but on the reality of oppression. These proposals recognize that this has always been a nation of dominant and dominated and that changing that pattern will require affirmative, nonneutral measures designed to make the least the most and to bring peace, at last, to this land.

In arguing for multiple consciousness as jurisprudential method, I do not mean to swoop up and thereby diminish the power of many different outsider traditions. Our various experiences are not coextensive. I cannot pretend that I, as a Japanese American, truly know the pain of, say, my Native- American sister. But I can pledge to educate myself so that I do not receive her pain in ignorance. And I can say as an American that I am choosing as my heritage the 200 years of struggle by poor and working people, by Native Americans, by women, by people of color for dignified lives of this nation. I can claim as my own the Constitution my father fought for at Anzio, the Constitution that I swore to uphold and defend when I was admitted to the bar. It was not written for me, but I can make it my own, using my chosen consciousness as a woman and person of color to give substance to those tantalizing words "equality" and "liberty."

These remarks are entitled "When the First Quail Calls" in reference to a signal used on the underground railroad to mark the time of departure to freedom. I imagine the fear and the courage of slaves who dared to leave the South and the fear of free Blacks and whites who chose to help them. They were all ahead of their time in thinking they could run a freedom train in the darkest hour of slavery.

Timing is an element of jurisprudential inquiry. How much can we hope to attain at this moment? When is it time to assert a new principle of law? When is it time to openly defy law? When is it time to sit and wait? Again we can look to the histories of oppressed groups to inform this inquiry. We can know that often it is time to set out on the freedom trail when the darkness is still upon us. You who are in law school now are stereotyped as the children of the Reagan era, concerned with economic success and uninvolved in political struggle. It is not the time, the commentators decree, for activism. And yet you set your own time. Students across the country are organizing conferences like this one, battling for affirmative action and divestment,[2] confronting racism and patriarchy, and listening in the night for the quail's call. I thank you for the honor of speaking to you and look forward to all we can learn from one another. We are the children of our pasts and the parents of our future. Like the Grimke sisters, we cannot listen to those who say, "It's not yet time." We know it is time, our time, and we will make it so.

1   Patricia Williams is a professor at Columbia Law School. Judy Scales-
     Trent is a professor at the State University of New York, Buffalo Law
     School. They were both speakers at the first annual Women of Color and
     the Law Conference.

2   Students at Yale and other universities waged successful struggles to force
     their schools to drop all investments in companies that did business in
     South Africa before the end of apartheid. The divestment movement,
     part of an international economic boycott, helped hasten the liberation of
     South Africa. See, e.g., "Anti-Apartheid Protest at Yale Draws Arrests,"
     The Associated Press, 22 September 1986; and Fred Bayles, "New Student
     Activism Focuses on Old Issue," *The Associated Press*, 12 May 1985.

2

This chapter was a keynote address to the Minority Section of the American Association of Law Schools, delivered at a 1995 luncheon[1] honoring Professor Richard Delgado for his contributions to scholarship. Professor Delgado was one of the first legal scholars to write explicitly from the perspective of a person of color. His work, and the work of many of the professors gathered at the luncheon, represents the intellectual strengths of identity politics.

Why write as a Japanese-American woman? Why not just as a law professor?

When I started teaching, well-meaning colleagues urged me to mask identity. "Don't get ghettoized in women's issues. Don't write about race, you'll become known as partisan rather than scholarly." Unfortunately, the same advice is handed out to aspiring teachers today. "Don't let your politics show on your resumé." Just this year a professor on an appointments committee asked whether I knew of any women or people of color who were not doing race and gender "stuff." All the names I sent to him were of people writing in those areas, and, he suggested, "We have enough of that." To anyone who longs for recognition as just a law professor, I wish you well. You should keep coming to minority section activities anyway. I promise you that you will need us someday. To those of you who are claiming your identity in your work, I would like to share my responses to the anti-identity crowd.

First, let me summarize the naysayers. In addition to the well-meaning colleagues who bring career advice about staying out of the ghetto, various pundits, academics, politicians, and theorists from all over the political map are attacking the new scholarship of identity. PC bashing is old news, and the only news is how doggedly attached the media are to old news—the same story, again and again, about how the multicultural thought police are taking over the academy.[2] If we had a dollar for every time this claim pops up in the press, we could save the NAACP.[3]

In addition to this PC bashing, there is a seemingly sophisticated claim that theoretical, scholarly use of identity is a dead end. In polite terms, this theoretical turn decries nationalism, narrowness, polemics, essentialism, vulgarization, parochialism, balkanization, and sidetracking from the main theoretical issues. "All this talk about race is masking class difference" is one such line. In less polite terms, the anti-identity theorists talk about guilt tripping, mau-mauing, or, as one critic said of my work, "self-aggrandizing slop." To talk about who we are as relevant to what we believe, in this view, is self-absorbed, narcissistic, and boring as well as a bullying move to silence others.

You may have noticed an inversion in many of these claims. The old school – masked identities, dominant narratives passing for universal – is portrayed as open and ecumenical. Challenges to this hegemony are seen as bullying and balkanizing. "We all got along until they discovered their identity." The cluster of

African-American or Asian or Latino students huddling in the corner of the cafeteria is seen as excluding the roomful of Anglos, not vice versa.

Because these kinds of inverting attacks are so obviously a result of someone's inability to share power, it seems a waste of time to respond. The pathbreaking work in critical race theory, feminist theory, and gay and lesbian studies is the best refutation. "We can't turn our whole life into a response," a critical race theorist once said to me.

We have not. We have spent most of our time doing work in the communities we care about, doing the scholarship that is inspiring to us. Nonetheless, the critical chorus grows more insistent, confuses students, affects hiring decisions, and remains the darling of the media monopoly. In addition, there is a legitimate debate in progressive circles about the utility of identity as an organizing device and in forming political theory. A brief response is in order.

Why racial identity – why now? Because it is still a radical act to stand in my shoes and speak when someone who looks like me is not supposed to do what I do. This is resistance. None of us were supposed to become law professors, write books, teach elites, or speak with authority about the words and systems that were designed to keep our kin under control. Most of us are here because someone in our family decided we could do more with our lives than what our teachers, what the dominant culture, said we could do. We were not mentored by our law professors. We were not the assumed, the chosen. Our students are still unsure of our capabilities. I see it as a form of resistance to stand in the front of the room on the first day of class and introduce myself as a Japanese-American, a feminist, and your law professor.

I was raised in a culture of modesty. The Japanese say, do not be the *deru kugi*, the nail that sticks out, or you will get hit on the head. How do I reconcile this with talking about myself and my identity on the first day of class? First of all, passing is impossible. This may be news to some of our colleagues, but most of us know this is true. More important, who I am colors how I see the world, how I understand questions of law and justice. By claiming, exploring, and questioning my own identity in an explicit way, I seek truth, and I seek to encourage my students to do the same.

I can take on the cloak of the detached universal, but it is an uncomfortable garment. It is not me, and I do not do my best work wearing it. I seek self-liberation when I write from my particular stance. The most brilliant and moving work coming from our community represents the liberated voice. I hear amidst the click of your keyboards the amazing sound of people doing something they never thought they would be able to do: speaking with their own voices in their professional lives. I hear Español climbing out of the footnotes up into the text. I see references to sexual identity becoming part of the analysis, not just the anecdote. I feel rhythm sneaking out of the subtitles to shape the flow of paragraphs. We are so much the richer for this work. People are actually reading law review articles for a change, passing photocopies along to friends. Practicing lawyers, miles away from the academy, are reading critical race theory because it reads well. "There was nothing like this," they say, "when I was in law school."

The fact that much of the new scholarship reads so well invites the charge that it is lightweight, the academic equivalent of a Kwanzaa cookbook. This would be true if nationalist gestures were served up in place of hard, theoretical work. The writing speaks for itself. It is no accident that the works of critical race theory are among the most cited throughout the academy by judges, scholars, and textbook writers. The ideas have value, and they are new and provocative precisely because they come from identities previously kept in the closet. The tradition of self-criticism, much a part of the political and cultural practices many of us are familiar with, adds to the rigor of this work.

But enough said about the value of speaking in one's own voice. I would like to address the politics of it. "What about Eastern Europe?" someone is bound to ask when I say I do not think identity politics is a bad thing. I think this view misunderstands and, again, inverts history. It assumes that racial identity is the cause of racial division rather than a product of it.

Our culture, our identity, is not entirely of our own making. We participate in and act upon what we are handed by history. I am the granddaughter of immigrant toilers. I choose to remember this and to celebrate the survival, resilience, and culture of my people. The Japanese American Citizens League takes positions on immigrant rights and against internments and relocations – of the Navajo, the Haitians, and antiwar protesters in the 1970s – because of a deliberate choice to remember what was done to us and to forge a political identity around it. This is a choice not every Japanese-American makes. There is agency involved in the way one uses identity, but it is not completely autonomous from what history hands us.

So what about Eastern Europe? I am no area expert, but I do know this: it was the Cold War that armed this region to the teeth, and it is the ideology of militarism and patriarchy that teaches that might makes right. It is the lust for wealth, power, spatial conquest, and raw materials that has driven wars for as long as the record of history, and ethnic identity is used in this deadly game. It is not inevitable that cultural differences lead to political division. Too often "clan fighting" or "ethnic hatred" is an easy explanation for conflicts actually generated by colonialism, cold war militarism, or economic exploitation.

There is a political agenda to the balkanization line. If ethnic identity is the cause of ethnic strife, the solution is for everyone to stop claiming ethnic identity and be "just like me." This is an obvious move away from recognizing the effects of systems of domination like racism or class exploitation.

This is not to say that mau-mauing is a good thing. A regressive use of identity politics is one that seeks merely to reverse conditions of domination and put one's own group on top. What a useless exercise. Nowhere in the critical race theory literature will you find anyone doing this. It is interesting that the critique of vulgar nationalism is made anyway, without citation.

This, again, is an inversion. For some people, any attempt to discuss the particularities of experience must be for the purposes of creating a new domination. Us and Them, someone has to be the alpha dog. If you are talking about your people, it must be because you want to exclude my people. This is a massive projection, the kind of projection made by hangers-on of the old order. It is like the white South Africans who fantasized that the end of apartheid would mean a bloodbath of revenge, massive relocation of people from their homes, and brutalizing punishments for the old regime. The gentleness of what in fact is going on in South Africa today shows whose mind was really on brutality, whose heart held secrets of self-loathing.

No one is saying that all people of color think alike. Neither are we saying that our color is irrelevant to our intellectual development. It is not an either-or situation. Let me say it again plainly because there is such a will to disbelieve: it is not either-or. We live in a complex, dynamic world. For many of us the heritage and experience of being part of one or more oppressed groups in twentieth-century America is a rich part of our lives. From the food on our table, to the music we listen to as we drive, to the protests we march in, to the theory we struggle with, something resonates from the place we call home. This is not all we are, and not everyone who looks like us hears the same call. But it is there, it is real, and, as the young people say, get used to it.

I do not know of any other politics of social change that works other than the one that asks people to explore deeply their own location on the axes of power. Know where you stand, what your privileges are, and who is standing on your toes. And when you holler, "Get off of my toes!" look around at the others, some most unlike you, who are also stepped on. The vibrancy of gay/lesbian political activism, in these dark days for progressives in the United States, shows how this formula still works, however imperfectly, to get folks in their marching shoes.

In summary, vulgar nationalism – that is not what we do. Progressive identity politics – there is no other way. Am I guilt tripping colleagues? I can only succeed if they have something to feel guilty about. Who we are is no longer a secret. We gather as the minority section out of a sense of affinity and politics that is good for our souls, our digestion, and our work. The result, of late, is distinguished scholarship, seeking human liberation, and reaching a readership wider than any law professor ever dreamed possible.[4]

There resides, in our particularities, a new and profound universality. I believe that is where our work is headed, and I rejoice at such good company as we move toward that home.

---

1   American Association of Law Schools Minority Section Luncheon Address, New Orleans, January 1995, Professor Robin Barnes, Organizer.
2   See, e.g, Lynne V. Cheney, *Why Our Culture and Our Country Have Stopped Making Sense — and What We Can Do about It* (New York: Simon & Schuster, 1995).
3   The NAACP faced a serious fiscal crisis at the time of this speech.
4   For examples of critical race theory writing, see K. Crenshaw; N. Gotanda, G. Peller, and K. Thomas, *Critical Race Theory* (New York. The New Press, 1995).

3

WE THE PEOPLE

Jurisprudence in Color

In 1987, the Minority Section of the American Association of Law Schools had a nervous breakdown, the factional, interracial details of which are probably not as significant as the theoretical impasse it reflected. While the section broke down, a group of law professors of color met across town to get critical, to break down in the traditions of our ancestors. At this meeting, I met for the first time the scholars who would become my lifetime partners in a struggle to create a new legal theory that would put race at the center of analysis. The following year, Professor Drew Days agreed to take over the faltering Minority Section, and he organized a conference session[1] aimed at revitalization. This talk outlines the early work that became Critical Race Theory.

There is a separate jurisprudential tradition of people of color in America, a jurisprudence in color, if you will. First, however, a caveat. There is a danger of falsely universalizing our diverse experiences as people of color. Because I believe the greater error lies in denying our commonality, I will continue in this effort to conceptualize a jurisprudence in color.

What is the jurisprudential tradition that sets apart the emerging view of law developed by people of color? It encompasses several key elements: historical memory, duality, criticism, race consciousness, pragmatism, and utopianism. The methodology of this jurisprudence is grounded in the particulars of social reality and the experience of people of color. This method is consciously historical and revisionist, attempting to know history from the bottom—from the fear and namelessness of the slave, from the broken treaties of the indigenous Americans, and from the daily experience of racial hierarchy. Understanding history from the bottom has forced these scholars to sources often ignored: journals, poems, the records of practitioners, the rhetoric of intellectuals of color, oral histories, the writers' own experience of life in a hierarchically arranged world, and even to the dreams they dream at night in their sleep.[2]

This methodology, which rejects presentist, eurocentric descriptions of social phenomena, offers a unique description of law. The description is realist. It accepts the standard teaching of street wisdom: law is essentially political. It accepts as well the pragmatic use of law as a tool for social change and the aspirational core of law as the human dream of peaceable existence. If these views seem contradictory, that is consistent with another component of outsider jurisprudence—it is jurisprudence recognizing, struggling within, and utilizing contradiction, dualism, and ambiguity.

The world described by legal scholars of color is one infused with racism. This description ties law to racism, showing that law is both a product and a promoter of racism. Like the feminists who have shown that patriarchy has had its own march through history, related to but distinct from the march of class struggle, scholars of color have also shown how racism must be understood as a distinct phenomenon.

The hopeful part of the description offered by outsider theorists is the recognition of the vulnerability of racist structures. The few who have managed to subject the many to conditions of degradation have used a variety of devices, from genocide to liberal doublespeak, that reveal the deep contradictions and instability inherent in any racist organization of social life. All the sorrow songs of outsider jurisprudence are thus tempered by an underlying descriptive message of the possibility of human social progress.

This progress can lead to a just world free of existing conditions of domination. The prescriptive message of this jurisprudence offers signposts to guide our way there—the focus on effects. The need to attack the effects of racism in order to attack its deep, hidden, tangled roots characterizes outsider thinking about law. Outsiders thus search for what Anne Scales calls the "rachet principle"[3]—legal tools that have a progressive effect, defying the habit of neutral principles to disappoint. They have proposed rachetlike measures—including affirmative action, reparations, and the criminalization of racist propaganda—to eliminate existing effects of oppression. These exciting doctrinal moves had their genesis in communities of people of color. Such measures are best implemented through formal rules, formal procedures, and formal concepts of rights because informality and oppression are frequent fellow travelers.

This identifies another tendency in jurisprudence by people of color: pragmatism and bottom-line instrumentalism in the use of law to achieve social change. Recall the litigants and lawyers of color bringing case after case challenging manifestations of racism throughout the history of this country. We have the famous cases— *Plessy, Brown, Korematsu, Lau,*[4]—and the unknown cases that pepper the reporters of every state in this nation: cases of ordinary people who suffered some racist affront – a lying landlord, a surly theater usher, a biased employer – and chose to fight back. One of my fantasies is that someday we will put up bronze plaques in all the theaters, train stations, schools, factories, and offices where these people, with their lovely cacophony of African-American, Asian, Latino, and Native-American surnames, fought their legal fights.

Bringing these elements together offers a challenge to classical and critical jurisprudence and a vision of law unlike any other. The historical memory and consciousness of race allies us with realists, critical legal theorists, and legal historians of the instrumentalist and law-and-society schools. Frederick Douglass, as we know, was a legal realist before Oliver Wendell Holmes.

What sets the jurisprudence of color apart, however, from the various modernist and postmodernist schools is the pragmatism rooted in concrete political organizing. In this sense, the jurisprudence of color forms an uneasy alliance with neoformalists, liberal reformists, and civil libertarians in commitment to the use of the rule of law to fight racism and in an unwillingness to stand naked in the face of oppression without a sword, a shield, or at least a legal precedent in our hands. Scholars of color have attempted to articulate a theoretical basis for using law while remaining deeply critical of it.

As José Bracamonte pointed out in his foreword to the *Harvard Civil Rights – Civil Liberties* Minority Critique of Critical Legal Studies,[5] people of color cannot afford to indulge in deconstruction for its own sake. Our critique is goal oriented. The work produced by scholars of color ties pragmatic law reform to criticism and radical theory in a way no one on the jurisprudential scene, except for our feminist sisters, is doing.

Our alliance with feminism will be, I believe, most fruitful for us. Martha Minnow's recent foreword to the Supreme Court edition of the *Harvard Law Review*, like its esteemed predecessor, the "Civil Rights Chronicles," grapples with the ideas of difference, duality, and the tantalizing promise of law.[6] Out of the struggle to understand the ways in which mainstream legal consciousness is white, male, Christian, able-bodied, economically privileged, and heterosexual will come a legal theory more profound than any other we have seen emanating from Anglo-American law schools. I speak of nothing less than transcendence of the self-declared bankruptcy of modernist thought and of something as dear as peace, freedom, and justice — words our poets, organizers, and legal scholars have never been too shy to speak.

To close, let me offer a road map of the work we are doing and suggestions for what we need to do to develop the jurisprudence of color.

First, description tells the untold stories of experiences of people of color under law and documents the facts of both our contributions and our exclusion. Using lawyerly expertise in reading legal documents, we should mine the primary sources to describe the role of race in American legal history.

Next, doctrinal development and critique has a long history in the experience of people of color. This is the work that stretches and shapes legal categories and advocates particular legal results. We should resist the trap of downgrading descriptive and doctrinal work. This trap is particularly prevalent at elite law schools. Descriptive and doctrinal work is not second-class work. It is work that in itself presents a sophisticated theoretical position, namely, that a legal response to the immediate needs of oppressed communities is a valuable method for deriving a theory of law and justice.

That brings us to the final category: theory. As phase one of the theoretical project, we need to critique the texts of law—cases, casebooks, law review articles, and jurisprudence monographs—to show how mainstream writers fail to account for racism and the experience of outsiders. You no doubt have a favorite article in the critique genre, and I want to beg for more. Where are our critiques, for example, of the standard textbooks used in the law schools?

The second stage of our theoretical work—theory building—will follow from critique. From identifying what is missing from standard jurisprudence it follows that we have ideas about what to fill in. We are here in the particular physical sense of our personal genealogies because we are the children of survivors, of people who judged correctly which fights to fight, when to lay low, and when to assert personhood. We are the children of generations before us who refused to accept the message of racial inferiority. Now I come dangerously close to privileging our experience in a way that is false. There are mistakes and villains in our histories. What I intend to suggest is only that there is something about life on this side of the color line that has theory-building potential. There is a reason that Justice Thurgood Marshall understands things not only about people of color but also about women, poor people, homosexuals, the physically disabled, and other outsiders that his colleagues in all their intelligence often fail to understand. It is not that being Black is a prerequisite to this understanding, as Justice Brennan demonstrates; rather, I want to identify and tap the source of Justice Marshall's vision that is related to his experience as a Black person.

Tapping that source is what jurisprudence is all about: the search for justice. The search for justice in the nuclear age carries an urgency previously unknown to humankind. As lawyers and theorists, let us go swiftly to our own histories and bring back to the law schools the truths we find there.

---

1   American Association of Law Schools Minority Section, Miami, Florida, January 9, 1988.

2   See Derrick Bell, "The Civil Rights Chronicles," *Harvard Law Review* 90 (1985): 4; Charles Lawrence, "The Word and the River: Pedagogy as Scholarship as Struggle," *Southern California Law Review* 65 (1992): 2231; and Patricia Williams, *Alchemy of Race and Rights* (Cambridge: Harvard University Press, 1991).

3   AALS Jurisprudence Section newsletter, December 1987, p. 5.

4   *Plessy v Ferguson*, 163 US 537 (1896) (upholding a law requiring separate railway accommodations for whites and Blacks); *Brown v Board of Education*, 347 US 483, 495 (1954) (holding that "[s]eparate educational facilities are inherently unequal and that laws requiring or permitting racial segregation of schools violate equal protection"); *Korematsu v United States*, 323 US 214 (1944) (upholding the internment of Japanese Americans during World War II on the ground of military necessity); and *Lau v Nichols*, 414 US 563 (1974) (holding that the school system's failure to provide English instruction to Chinese-American students with limited English proficiency violated equal protection).

5   José Bracamonte, Foreword, "Minority Critiques of the Critical Legal Studies Movement," *Harvard Civil Rights–Civil Liberties Law Review* 22 (1982): 297.

6   Martha Minnow, "Justice Engendered," *Harvard Law Review* 101 (1987): 10.

4

*Property is a notion that sits above all others in the American legal tra-
dition. Teachers of property law face a monumental task because so much
of the law deals with property. The typical first-year course gallops across
an array of topics, cases, and precedents. One thing property professors
have not always thought about is gender. In 1990, the Property Section
of the American Association of Law Schools, in one of its best attended
conference presentations, opened the floor to feminists. These remarks
were part of the proceedings.*

Let me begin by stepping back a bit from the expansiveness of
our discussion to try to situate what feminists and critical race
theorists are doing in the recent intellectual history of the academy. Historian Gerda Lerner suggested two stages of feminist
history that are analogous to developments in law.[1] In describing feminist historiography, first, she says, we tried to recover
lost women, to show how the lives of women impacted history.
Second, she says, we moved beyond mere description of
women's roles. In the second stage, we attempted to retheorize,
redefine, and reanalyze – to take what we learned about women
in history and use it to reconceive the very notion of history.

From the descriptive time lines of great events, to the explanations of why events happened, to the subdivisions of historical knowledge within which we locate our explanation, bringing women into the picture altered everything.

Similarly, in law, the first prescient scholars to bring feminism to the law schools started courses called "women and the law" and "sex discrimination." This was the crucial, first stage of describing the impact of law on women and of describing women's exclusion. These courses were often organized like courses in property law in that they took something called "women" and went through the places in law that touch women: women and crime, women and family, and women and employment.

From looking at these instances of law interacting with gender, we moved naturally into the second stage of understanding law as attached structurally to a historical force called patriarchy. By "patriarchy," I mean the social system that assigns cultural characteristics to the male and female sexes and uses that characterization, along with other instruments of power (including state power), to perpetuate the subordination of female to male.[2]

What does this have to do with the law of property? At the first stage, we can ask questions about property law in relation to subordinated groups. Women and people of color are disproportionately poor and therefore underpropertied; they are tenants, or homeless, or living in substandard housing. They face difficulty in access to housing, segregation, insurance redlining, steering, Jim Crow, blockbusting, and move-in violence – practices that are shockingly alive and well even as we celebrate twenty-five years under the civil rights acts. The reality of sexual use and abuse of women means that women are sexually harassed by landlords and that women are regularly assaulted by criminals in residential settings, often without redress in law. A first-stage look at property law might ask, Are we paying adequate attention to these intersections of property, law, and the lives of women and people of color?

In the second stage, the methodology of feminism and critical race theory suggests new insights into our very understanding of property. Feminists and people of color in law are using new methods of legal analysis. There is a tendency in this work to look at the small, at personal experience, at absences. Whose voice is missing from a conversation? What aspects of human life do we *not* have laws for? What calls do the police *not* answer? Starting from the lived experience of women and people of color, asking these kinds of questions leads to larger theoretical questions: Why is a particular legal conception seen as immutable? Why the privileged position of property in our legal system? Who defines property? How is law related to patriarchy?

Applying this method to the law of property is rich with promise for theoretical insight, whether or not one accepts the liberation struggles that produce it. Just as Marxist analysis can provide insight for non-Marxists, say, into the relationship between the Industrial Revolution and changes in nuisance laws, so can feminists and people of color suggest analysis useful to all seekers of knowledge, regardless of ideology.

Look at the nineteenth century. Look for the absences and systems of subordination. Who was landless? Who could not own land? What was defined as property? How were women, children, and enslaved Africans treated as property, and what did that mean in the concrete reality of their lives? How were attitudes toward property structured in the thought of cultural subgroups: white men, white women, Black men, Black women,

Native-American men, Native-American women, frontier homesteaders, and eastern land barons? How was land lost, and from whom and to whom? How did law facilitate this process?

Even though our own time has seen a decline in letter writing, novel reading, independent newspapers, and the saving of texts, the nineteenth century is our most richly documented in terms of a written record of the lives of ordinary people. We have hundreds of slave narratives, local newspapers, pioneer diaries, mother-daughter letter collections, and widely read popular magazines and novels. From the old archives, attitudes toward property emerge.

The slave narratives reveal a bitter understanding of the injustice of people as property and knowledge that the category "property" in the slave states was both stable and unstable. It was stable in the sense that treating human beings as chattel was seen as necessary to the economy and was firmly entrenched in legal codes. It was unstable in that human beings are not suitable for the status of property. They think and feel and rebel and cause empathy in others. Reading both the slave codes and slave narratives shows that this instability was recognized all around. The legal system of slavery, then, was under constant threat of disintegration, an example of the law of ownership as historically contingent and the concept of property as mutable.

In addition to owning other human beings, white men owned land. As owners and would-be owners of property, they crystallized the romance of the fee simple[3] in the nineteenth century. Freedom, individualism, and ambition were tied to a lust for land of one's own. The language of domination and conquest marks discussion of property in this period: to conquer the American desert; to penetrate the virgin prairie; to stake, fence, mine, plow, build, expand, and own in absolute dominion. The men who used this language were, historians of the period tell us, frequently violent. Hunting, shooting, and brawling in the "no-holds-barred" style were common pastimes. On the frontier, torture of animals—bear baiting and gander pulling (decapitating greased geese with one's bare hands while on horseback) —were public sports. Catharine MacKinnon, in her work, sees violence against women as sine qua non of patriarchy.[4] Is it also central to patriarchal attitudes toward property? Is absolute dominion the perfect metaphor for the nineteenth-century male psyche?

White women had fascinating relationships to property. As you know, married women could not own property in their own name. Women suffered from a range of legal disabilities that the first generation of American feminists came to recognize and campaign against. White women were, in this age of clearly defined gender roles, less violent and less aggressive in both public and private life. They were more averse to change and risk. The wives who went on the westward migration went reluctantly, urged on and motivated by men. The women did share a lust for land, but their expression of it was different. They sat and cross-stitched the words "Home Sweet Home." They planted tansy by the doorstep to keep out ants. They swept, carded, spun, churned, washed, starched, prettied, and cared for children. Those who moved west longed to make the frontier look like the home they left, going so far as to hand-carry seeds and cuttings of familiar flowers across plain and mountain range. Domination was the end, but domestication was the means. This is how women, disabled from ownership, expressed their dominion in property.

Native-American men and women at first welcomed the immigrants, offering trade and aid to the wagon trains. The Native-American concept of property focused on use, not ownership. More important, Native Americans understood property as bearing personality. Margaret Radin has noted that western cultures sometimes lodge personhood in property.[5] In Native-American culture, the property itself had personhood. Land and nature operated by a logic and power entitled to deference, care, reciprocation, and sometimes fear and trembling. Understanding the Native view, preserved in the oral tradition and resource practices emanating from the hundreds of Native cultures of the United States, is useful to students of property. In teaching the history of property law to my students, I like to point out that the concept of the fee simple absolute is a pea in the Pacific Ocean in relation to the history of human conceptions of property.

Understanding that ideas about property change over time, across cultures, and across gender helps students understand the logic and the internal tensions in the common law of property. Whether our relation to land is one of dominance and control or humility and stewardship is the fundamental question of the postindustrial world: Professor Williams asked in the pages of the *Harvard Civil Rights – Civil Liberties Law Review* whether we want to own the gold or to let a golden spirit own us.[6] In her writing she talks about property as a status, of being owned and owning in a way that challenges legal thinking. I recommend her writing to teachers of property.

As writers like Patricia Williams and my copanelists here today are writing theory to take us into the twenty-first century, they are joined by others asking new questions about property. Professor John Calmore is asking how public housing policy has perpetuated racism and poverty.[7] Ecofeminists have suggested that a feminine ethic of care and holistic intersubjectivity must mark our relationship to property if we are to survive as a species in the nuclear age. Other feminist writers might challenge what they see as the essentialism in such arguments. These ideas may sound strange, discordant, and difficult to you, just as Archie Shepp's music sounds difficult to me. I am still listening to Archie Shepp because I have found that it is good exercise to listen to what I do not quite understand. I hope those of you who choose to consider the new works on jurisprudence and property emanating from women and people of color enjoy the exercise.

In the paradigm of Blackacre lives a gender icon, a male. He holds a gun and can use reasonable force to keep out intruders. He owns title, a legal shell creating boundaries you may not cross without his permission. In that shell there lives a woman, too. The space in which she dwells is called private. From that space she reaches out and asks, "What has property meant to me?"

If she owns it, too, she is the ultimate equal in the eyes of the law. Does the bundle of rights to use, lease, exploit, sell, and exclude mean she is now free? For the thousands of women abused and assaulted in their own homes, the legal shell excluding strangers is not the ultimate sign of liberty and personhood the law imagines.

This is a thought about property that began in the battered women's shelters and that may make it to your casebooks. More important, it may make it to the gate at Blackacre, rewriting the cultural code of dominion, violence, and private shells, creating newer properties of equality and safety for women.

1   See Gerda Lerner, *Black Women in White America: A Documentary History* (New York: Pantheon Books, 1972).

2   This systemic definition of patriarchy is similar to the definition of racism as it is used in critical race theory.

3   "Fee simple" is a legal term for complete ownership of property, characterized by the ability to exclude others and to pass the property on to one's heirs.

4   See Catharine MacKinnon, "Feminism, Marxism, Method, and the State: Toward Feminist Jurisprudence," *Signs* 8 (1983): 635, and *Feminism Unmodified: Discourses on Life and Law* (Cambridge: Harvard University Press, 1989).

5   See Margaret Rading, "Market Inalienability," *Harvard Law Review* 100 (1987): 1849.

6   Patricia Williams, "Alchemical Notes: Reconstructed Ideals from Deconstructed Rights," *Harvard Civil Rights – Civil Liberties Law Review* 22 (1987): 401.

7   See John Calmore, "Fair Housing vs. Fair Housing: The Problems with Providing Increased Housing Opportunities through Spatial Deconcentration," *Clearing-House Review* 14 (1980): 7, and "Racialized Space and the Culture of Segregation: Hewing a Stone, Hope from a Mountain of Despair," *University of Pennsylvania Law Review* 143 (1995): 1233.

5

When Congress passed a new crime bill in 1994, the editors of Ms. *magazine wanted a legal scholar to analyze the legislation from a feminist perspective. In reading and critiquing the crime bill, I soon realized that feminists needed to take on the notion of crime writ large to understand crime as a feminist issue.*

I remember the strangeness of my mother's early warnings about dangerous men. She was a preschool teacher who extolled making friends, sharing, and respecting the feelings of others. She taught me songs in different languages and brought home multicultural paper dolls. She wanted me to go bravely out into the world and love its many peoples. In light of this, her sharp voice startled me the time we were stopped at a red light and I waved back at a man who waved at me from inside a bar. I knew I was safe there in the car with my mother. But she did not think I was safe.

She said, "What are you doing? You don't know that man. You can't be friendly with men you don't know because some men are bad, and they will want to hurt you." She used the serious, instructive voice that meant danger—a good mother teaching her daughter caution and fear.

All women fear crime. A consciousness-raising tool I use with women students is to ask them about their fears of bodily harm. We find a commonality that crosses race and class lines — all women know they are potential targets in a country that favors power, violence, and the objectification of women. No woman old enough to read this article has survived this far in life without engaging in the daily rituals of crime avoidance under patriarchy. There are places we do not go, strangers we withhold information from, quick strides in the parking lot that say, "Don't mess with me." There are locks, alarms, whistles, and, in my case, a large dog. Students tell me they have stayed in mediocre relationships because, among other things, they fear the vulnerability of living alone and female. Among patriarchy's many crimes is the crime that keeps us from going out alone on an evening stroll to look at the stars. This is a real loss of personal freedom. This is a feminist issue.

If crime is a feminist issue, what are we to make of the resurgence of crime as the number one concern in mainstream politics? One clue is that the enemies of feminism — from the lynch mobs of the nineteenth century to the Nixon/Reagan/Bush cadres of the twentieth — have always run on the "crime is everywhere, we need real men in charge" platform.

In 1994, Washington offered us yet another get-tough crime bill: new crimes, more death penalty, more prisons, and more cops. This is what we got from a president who promised us health care, social programs, and jobs. Whether or not he was stymied, as he claims, by his enemies and detractors, he loves the crime bill as much as the next do-nothing politician. "I care about you, I got you the crime bill."

This crime bill included provisions feminists lobbied for. The Violence Against Women Act, with its command to take crimes against women seriously, is seen by many as progressive. When I was in law school, I listened to a lecture by a visiting prosecutor who said he would not try a rape case unless the women had bruises – or at least missing buttons and torn underwear. He would not say this today. It was feminism that pushed prosecutors to take rape and domestic violence seriously. Our rape crisis centers, our shelter workers, our courtroom monitors, our protests, and our lobbying of state legislatures forced changes in the treatment of crimes against women.

Congress has now brought this change to the national level in the latest crime bill. As a feminist, however, I cannot celebrate crime legislation that advances the protection of women without providing for racial justice. I cannot rejoice at crime legislation that is the deadliest in American history, horrifically expanding the list of capital crimes. Unlike most of the women in Congress, I would not have voted for this crime bill.

I remember sitting in a meeting called by the Center for Women's Policy Studies, discussing the Violence Against Women Act. Would I have to be the first to say it? No – there in that room full of activists, academics, and professional agitators were other women, including white women, who expressed their anger about the rates of imprisonment of African-American men.

Could I support legislation that would give yet another tool to police and prosecutors? I thought of the young Asian teenagers in southern California who are photographed by the police every time they go to the mall, their portraits collected in "mug books" to help identify "potential gang members." I thought of my brother, frantically trying to explain to the police, "We're just students, college students at UCLA," while his brown-skinned friend lay face down on a Westwood sidewalk with an LAPD gun held to his head.

I knew that, in many communities I care about, the police are a source of crime and violence as well as a deterrent to it. I knew that any new penalties for violence against women would disproportionately imprison men of color. This is not because men of color commit more crimes against women; contrary to the popular lie, they do not. They do, however, stand in the places where the system chooses its favorites for punishment. Since 1930, close to 90 percent of those executed for rape in this country were African American. This genocidal history of selective enforcement is a wrenching concern, as is the violence against women of color that is too often ignored both within and without our communities. As feminists formulated a position on the Violence Against Women Act, it was necessary, as it often is in feminist practice, to do two things at once: demand effective prosecution of crimes against women and demand restructuring of the criminal justice system to end racist enforcement practices.

A key first step in that direction was the Racial Justice Act. That bill would have commanded the evenhanded application of the death penalty in response to the historical reality of race as a key factor in determining who is executed.

Requiring equality in the application of the death penalty is an unholy demand: kill them equally. The Racial Justice Act was, however, an important public recognition of racism in the criminal justice system. It is both a sadness and a shame that Congress could not even say this: we will not kill you unless we can do it without racial bias.

I live in a country where politicians will not say this. That being true, what am I to make of the crime bill? I read the metro section of the paper every morning and see reasons to lock my door and write off segments of the human family. I read of men who do incomprehensible violence to wives and lovers and children and strangers. I know that until we have gone the long road to the place where all children grow up loved and cared for, where the meanness of patriarchal culture is replaced with the loving culture feminists imagine possible, there will live among us those who are irreparably damaged and viciously dangerous.

For now, feminists must dance with the devil — demanding that the existing criminal justice system protect women from violence even as we criticize and work toward the abolishment of that system. This requires long discussions about practical politics as well as deep theory.

We need to ask how patriarchy has governed our thinking about crime. Current anticrime rhetoric is about "power over"; we must get power over criminals before they get power over us. It reminds me of my neighbors who douse their lawns with herbicides — chemical relations to the deadly Agent Orange — to kill the sweet violets, the wild strawberries, and the exuberant crabgrass that invade East Coast lawns. It reminds me of the real Agent Orange, dumped on rain forests that hid peasants who wished only to grow their rice in peace. It reminds me of war, patriarchy's dispute resolution mechanism, that which we have such a hard time explaining to our children when they ask, "But why? Why is there war?"

Here is the patriarchal model: Do not do that, or we will hurt you, lock you up, kill you, and if that does not work, we will triple the penalties and come after you with more guns. Used against sweet violets, this model poisons the grass our children play on. Used against the children themselves, it turns them into adults you would not want near anyone you care about. Alas, the crime bill includes new ways of criminalizing children as young as thirteen by treating them as adult offenders.

Any intelligent person in the business of locking up criminals will tell you it is not working. From the embittered cop on the beat to Janet Reno, the nation's highest prosecutor, anyone with a real eye on crime knows we do not have power over it, and we never will. We could never hire enough cops, build enough prisons, multiply enough penalties, or lock up enough teenagers to prevent crime through the patriarchal model. This is the first feminist critique: Get-tough tactics do not prevent crime.

Politicians fear the label "soft on crime." I hear homophobia whispering here, "Don't be a sissy, vote for the crime bill." What embitters and enrages me is that those who supported the bill know it will not work. In response to our legitimate fears, they offered fraudulent gimmicks, like "three strikes you're out," when all the evidence before them showed that such gimmicks do not make us safer.

It is the things we have asked for all along that will stop crime: quality child care and paid parental leave, guaranteed minimum income, universal literacy, affirmative action, and free health care, including mental health care and drug rehabilitation programs. The meager, window-dressing social programs in the original crime bill were taken out, leaving only the patriarchal model. We have to say, loudly, that the politicians who gave us more punishment and no prevention are the cause of the inevitable next wave of crime that will hit our streets.

The critique of the patriarchal model extends beyond its patent ineffectiveness. In addition to doing nothing about crime, this model actually generates it. When we execute murderers, we teach that the power of the state to destroy is awesome. It is something to fear, envy, and emulate. When we send armed police into grade schools and housing projects, we teach the children that guns equal power, that the powerful get guns. If you do not like it, smash it. Our city carnage, the young bodies, the blood on the sidewalk – we taught our children this.

We are raped because men learn in this culture that the degradation of women is normal. We are battered because men learn in this culture that disregard of human pain is a hallmark of power. The criminal justice system, as represented in this recent crime bill, does nothing to change this culture because it is part of it. It is part of the dehumanization of young people that makes them care little for their own lives, much less for the lives of others. It is part of the kill-what-scares-you ideology of patriarchy that is war, is lynching, is gay bashing, is over fifty new death penalty offenses in the crime bill.

A couple of years ago, I went back to the park where I played as a child and was shocked to find it completely denuded of trees. The giant sycamores and eucalyptus that had made it an oasis in city-center Los Angeles were all gone. I remembered the sense of ownership I felt for those trees – my trees, my park, where I saw the amazing sights of the world my mother sent me out into: black teenagers playing the dozens, Chicana girls in wedding-cake first-communion dresses, Jewish girls who knew the names of all the Dodgers, and everywhere transistor radios playing Aretha. The young and the bold gathered and mixed there in the multicultural paradise of my memory, the air heavy with the scent of eucalyptus.

Today the park is empty, the swings are still, and the trees are gone. I asked a cousin about this, and he said they cut down the trees so the cops could scan the park when they drive by. Whether the drugs preceded the defoliation or followed it, I do not know, but I do know that we could kill every tree in every park and still have crime.

Treeless parks, three-strikes-you're-out, and the Violence Against Women Act, and we are not safe.

Feminists cannot afford reaching for less than the utopian. We should demand, now, community control of police and prosecutors. Feminists, families from the projects, lesbians and gay men, and representatives of all groups with a stake in bringing fairness to police practices should sit on review boards with actual hiring and firing power and they should fill the ranks of law enforcement from top to bottom. Early reports show that women often make better cops.[1] They can defuse volatile situations and are less frequently involved in brutality.

The primary demands of the feminist cause – decent education, jobs, housing, and health care for all – must remain our organizing priority. The generalized crime that hurts all and that hurts especially those with limited resources is a product of social injustice. It is the gulf between the "haves" and the "have-nots" that causes crime. If you do not believe me, take a tour of the countries in which this gulf is most acute (ours included) and see how the rich live behind barricades while the poor live in chaos.

The particular crime that women face is something we need long, deep talks about. Gay and lesbian bashing and racist and anti-Semitic hate crimes are escalating. There is increasing evidence that rape, the antiwomen hate crime, is also increasing. Many of us share a sense of heightened physical danger directly related to our demands for equality. Like all forms of backlash, this one is a sign that we are both winning and at risk.

My mother raised her daughter in paradox. Be fearless, she said. Be whatever you want to be; go wherever you want to go. Be fearful, she said. Some men are bad, and they will want to hurt you. There are things you cannot do and places you cannot go. Because her house was a house of love, this dual message did not make me crazy. It made me strong.

The lessons of paradox are the lessons of survival under patriarchy. In approaching crime, feminists must make alternative and conflicting demands. When they refuse to prosecute crimes against us, we must march to the police station and demand that they act. When they execute anyone, for whatever horrible crime, we must march to the gallows and say, "Not in our names." When the cops will not come when a mom calls to complain about the dealer on the corner, we have to stand with her and demand protection, even as we call for an end to police crimes in the same neighborhood.

All women fear crime, and the crime we fear will not end until patriarchy ends. The crime bill I am waiting for is the one that enacts the feminist wish list. In the meantime, go on to your self-defense class and talk to strangers about organizing a third party.

---

1 See, e.g. *Report of the Independent Commission on the Los Angeles Police Department*, 9 July, 1991, p. 84 (suggesting that "female officers . . . are not nearly as likely to be involved in use of excessive force" and that they are "more communicative, more skillful at de-escalating potentially violent situations and less confrontational").

6

Professor Kimberlé Williams Crenshaw began calling what radical law professors of color were doing "critical race theory" when she organized a retreat at a spartan, convent in the summer of 1989. It was "critical" both because we criticized and because we respected and drew on the tradition of postmodern critical thought then popular with left intellectuals. It was "race" theory because we were, both by personal circumstance and through our understanding of history, convinced that racism and the construction of race were central to an understanding of American law and politics. As legal theory, critical race theory uncovers racist structures within the legal system and asks how and whether law is a means to attain justice. This essay was an initial response to Professor Crenshaw's call for a critical theory of race and law.

PROLOGUE: ACTING YOUR COLOR

I was one of a group of nine-year-old girls sitting on a bench out on the hot, treeless playground of Queen Anne Place Elementary School in city-center Los Angeles. We were sitting and waiting—maybe for a bell to ring, maybe because a playground supervisor had "benched" us. Meaningless waiting was not something we questioned. A Black girl at the end of the bench was acting silly, jostling and shouting. We were sitting close on that bench, so another Black girl decided to take on the part of the grownup. She said in a slow, wise, commanding voice, "Girl, stop acting your color." The words struck me, a child raised to watch for racism, like a truck.

I thought and thought about those words and have never gotten them out of my mind. How could children, so young, know there is such a thing as acting one's color, that it is bad, that it is the opposite of waiting quietly, that calling attention to oneself is dangerous, that color carries a burden of correct behavior and a risk of judgment by another, more powerful world? In what ways is this related to the danger of *not* acting one's color—the danger of punishment for refusing to remain childish and for showing one's strength, judgment, and maturity? I am sure my bossy nine-year-old benchmate grew up to walk into that wall more than once.

When children who are conscious of race and danger from the time of their earliest memories grow up to become lawyers, do they think and feel differently from other lawyers? Yes, yes they do.

Introduction

Like cactus flowers after a rain in the Mojave, strange, bright writing popped up in the law reviews in the 1980s. People of color, writing in their own voices, presented a conception of law different from any other—a conception so complete and unique that it comprised a new jurisprudence. This new jurisprudence was deeply critical of law as an enforcer of racist maldistributions of wealth and power, and yet it diverged from the thought of postmodern legal thinkers who argued the disutility of law as a tool of progressive social change. This new jurisprudence was born of scholars who were cynically hopeful. They – being radical people of color housed in law schools – were not even supposed to exist, yet they did. Perhaps they took their own lives as evidence that anything is possible.

What's Going On?

In the fall of 1985, the *Harvard Law Review* published Derrick Bell's "Civil Rights Chronicles" as the foreword to its Supreme Court issue.[1] The prestigious designation of foreword authorship had never before produced such an unusual piece of writing. With a tone of dead seriousness, Bell wrote of an encounter with an apparition. Bell told a story. He abandoned the law review form, using instead fantasy, narrative, and dialogue to tell a bitter tale of law. Some thought this a self-indulgent and bizarre act. Others described it as brilliant, moving, and incisive. These early mixed reviews bear telling resemblance to first accounts of any new art form, including various stages of American jazz.

Soon after, Charles Lawrence published an account of a dream of his in which he confronted a racist white law professor and discovered "the significance of fear."[2] The conceptualization of fear as a motivational force in life and in law – intertwined with a critique of meritocratic legal lies, all in a short account of one man's dream – was stunning to readers who identified with Lawrence's experience. Fans of Lawrence's work made copies to send to wounded academic friends for the balm that comes from knowing that one's pain is not merely one's own pain.

The numbers of legal academics of color who felt alienated from existing legal discourse became clear when a call for critical scholars of color went out in 1986. About thirty law professors of color attended caucuses at the Los Angeles Critical

Legal Studies[3] Conference, and six presented major addresses.[4] The 1986 Critical Legal Studies conference theme, "The Sounds of Silence," was intended to recover absent voices. The six speakers worked separately in cities distant from one another. Most had never met the others but were aware of the works of Bell and Lawrence. From these six speakers, representing different racial and geographic communities, came a remarkably similar critique of critical legal studies. Every speaker commented on the marginalization of the experience of people of color in postmodern legal theory and on the way in which the critique of rights failed to account for the understanding of rights and racism emanating from subordinated communities.

Although the speakers themselves were impressed by the parallels in their separate voices, the audience was deeply divided. Some, mostly feminists, expressed empathy for the race-generated critique of the critique of rights. Others felt the new ideas misunderstood and unfairly maligned the critical legal studies movement. Several in attendance reported heated debates, tears, and anger emerging in various conference sessions.

The debate widened as some of the conference presentations were published in the *Harvard Civil Rights – Civil Liberties Law Review* and elsewhere. Students of color were among the first to discover these new writers and to invite the writers to address student groups. A resurgence of student activism resulted in new pushes for affirmative action hiring and for conferences devoted to race issues. Sit-ins, rallies, and guerilla actions were reported at Boalt, Stanford, Harvard, and Columbia. The circle of young, critical scholars of color arguing and writing grew.

Is That Jazz?

The new jurisprudence is characterized by its methodology, description of law, and prescription for social change. This section responds to those who ask whether the work of progressive legal scholars of color really constitutes a jurisprudence. Although delineating critical race theory risks slighting the diversity and complexity of the voices it comprises, it is important to acknowledge a common ground. To acknowledge that a liberationist intellectual movement exists – to name it and to include it in discussions at the centers of learning – is a political act.

METHOD   The method of derivation and presentation of critical race theory is marked by consciousness of the history and experience of subordinated people. Using stories, testimonials, and accounts of personal and mythical experience, writers of color evoke a worldview that challenges the status quo in legal thought. Thus stories appear in the body and the footnotes of the new legal writing. Stories are exchanged in caucuses and at conferences and rescued up from nontraditional sources: oral history, poems, dreams, memory, and genealogy.

Contrasting the understanding of law derived from these stories with the understanding derived from traditional legal sources makes for dramatic tension as well as jurisprudential enlightenment. Like feminist consciousness raising, this use of storytelling creates a tension between a tale of oppression and a tale of innocence, leading to only two possible conclusions: someone is lying, or someone is deeply deluded.

The liberal, process-oriented vision of legal institutions moving clumsily toward a goal of equality and inclusion is undermined through tale after tale of people of color victimized by law, law schools, and legal institutions. One side says racism is an isolated, waning phenomenon, soon to succumb to legal tools promoting equality. The other side says racism is a pervasive, resilient phenomenon, supported and masked by legal tools promoting equality.

DESCRIPTION   The abstract philosopher's question in jurisprudence is, What is law? The concrete reality of people of color suggests a characteristically dualist answer. It takes a version of the realist/critical answer: law is an instrument of political power used to privilege ruling elites. It then adds two twists. The first twist is the central role of racism in American law. Using historical and personal accounts of racism, these scholars show the ways in which the law supports racism and the degree to which racism contributes to the development of law in the United States. The second twist is derived from the experience of struggle. The struggle against racism is historically a struggle against and within law. The hard-won victories of that struggle demonstrate the duality of law: law as subordination and law as liberation.

Thus the "everything is up for grabs" description of critical legal studies becomes "change is possible; there is a reward for constant struggle" when mediated through the history of abolitionist and antiracist movements. Writers like Richard Delgado, Kimberlé Crenshaw, Charles Lawrence, and Patricia Williams offer at once a deeply critical voice and a voice cognizant of the role law plays in the struggle for human liberation. They suggest that rights, formality, and rules are more than shuttlecocks in a game of law-reform badminton. They are deadserious promises broken at the expense of human well-being.

American law is born of racism and gives birth to racism. Law thus becomes a locus of struggle. Struggle can change law, and law can aid struggle. We have seen, in our communities, people willing to pay with their lives for change in legal relations—to bring a more progressive legalism into their communities and to take racism out. This legacy leads to a description of law as a part of progressive movements.

A jurisprudence includes a definition of justice. What is justice according to critical race theory?

It is antiracist.

It is substantive.

It is attainable.

Critical race theory, grounded as it is in a descriptive understanding of racism as a resilient, antiprogressive force in American history, suggests that an antiracist agenda is key to a conception of justice. Ending racism through law is an immediate prescriptive agenda, as is ending all forms of subordination.

A just world is one that heals the wounded among us, that brings back the lost and the wasted, that elevates all human beings to their highest potential. The only way to do this is through a substantive conception of rights. In addition to the language of process and equality familiar in liberal discourse, scholars of color add a language of entitlement and community.

Entitlement: each human being is entitled, in this rich nation of ours, to the material means to attain a decent life.

Community: the broader community has both special obligation to disadvantaged communities and affirmative duties to reverse longstanding patterns of exploitation and maldistribution. Only then can the entire community flourish.

Thus, these scholars call for nonneutral, asymmetrical concepts of law, such as affirmative action. Such prescriptions make sense only if one starts from a belief that subordination exists, that racism and other instruments of domination are widespread, and that advantage and disadvantage have little to do with merit and a lot to do with systemic, institutionalized oppression.

Whether one believes this depends on one's conceptualization of intent and causation. The focus of the new jurisprudence is on effects. The writers frequently use statistical and anecdotal evidence to show the subordinated status of people of color in America and reject a linear, intent-based notion of causation. If the effects of racism exist, that is cause for action. As Charles Lawrence noted in one of the definitive articles of the emerging critical race theory genre, whether anyone intended that effect is largely irrelevant in a world of multiple causation and unconscious racism.[5]

The prescription, then, derives directly from the description, which derives in turn from the method of hearing the voices from the bottom, contrasted with the voices from the top. Legal intellectuals of color are not the only ones who can do this, but they do tend to do this more often than most legal scholars.

The prescription is an emotional one. Critical race theorists remind us that there are real human lives touched by law. They use the first person and speak of their parents, their children, their kin, and their daily lives. Their jurisprudence is also, in spite of a deeply critical stance, an optimistic one. Who but an optimist, after all, would see American racism and choose to write about it instead of conceding to its strength in preacknowledged defeat? That they write, enter theoretical debate, teach in law schools, speak to white audiences, and participate in community struggle is all a testimony of faith. The irony of their rejection as divisive, separatist, and impolitic is that if they were those things they would not be doing what they are doing.

Nobody Knows You When You're Down and Out

The critiques of the new jurisprudence are basically these:
   1. It does not exist.
   2. It is not unique to people of color.
   3. It is paranoid and separatist.
   4. It is rosy, superficial, and theoretically wrong.

First, one might argue, critical race theory is not a new jurisprudence. It does not carry the trappings of more formalized schools of thought: an organization, newsletter, institute, or endowed chair. People of color, critics suggest, do not all think alike any more than they all look alike. To suggest that a jurisprudence flows from being of a certain race is silly determinism and racist as well.

In response to the critique of nonexistence, there is something going on when several writers all come up with related ideas, deeply divergent from mainstream thought, and when the only commonality in their life experience is racism. Obviously not all legal scholars of color agree, nor do all the writers I allude to here agree on all things. Nonetheless, the points of agreement are striking.

If it is striking, the critique continues, it is hardly unique or original. White folks see racism, too. Critical scholars of color did not invent the critique of neutrality, the phenomenology of race, or any of the other components of their work.

Critical race theory is explicitly derivative of the history and intellectual tradition of people of color and responsive to developments in liberal and critical thought. It makes no claim of original invention, using instead a method that leads to discovery of experiences of racism and struggles in law longstanding in their communities. Of course, white scholars can tap these same sources.

Nonetheless, there is something identifiably unique in the recognition of race as a social force, the use of dualist tension and the method of storytelling in critical race theory writing. In time, we will look back and say with confidence, "This is a distinct body of theoretical work."

Is critical race theory paranoid and separatist? If coalition building is the key to political victory in the 1990s, writing perceived as antiwhite or as glorifying racial/ethnic consciousness is certainly not the way to proceed.

There is a value in occasional separatism, particularly when it results in people putting their wounds, secrets, and dreams on paper. This is an effort to communicate, not to separate. The readiness with which some will interpret collective acts and statements by people of color as divisive is itself an interesting comment on our learned ignorance and racial divisions. As one Black speaker chided me when I mistakenly complimented her on the "anger" in her speech, "If I were really angry, I wouldn't be talking here."

The need to form coalitions, to keep talking over the gulfs, and to risk rejection as we mis-hear one another is recognized in progressive circles. The critical legal studies movement braved organizing the minuet of elephants that cross-gender, interracial dialogue often resembles. White critical legal studies scholars wrote responses to the minority critique, treating it as real and substantial. Disagreements exist, but no one is proposing separatism.

A final and significant intellectual challenge to the new jurisprudence asks how one can walk the catwalk between rights and racism or, as Professor Kimberlé Crenshaw put it, reform and retrenchment.[6] Critical legal studies scholars, influenced by the collapse of the liberal law reform efforts of their lifetimes, have developed a sophisticated and deeply skeptical approach to rights and legalism. To hear scholars of color say, "In spite of the critique of legalism, we still remember with hope and pride the legal victories of the civil rights movement," sounds naive and ill-informed, the blind hope for change that is the victim's prize.

Some scholars of color will concede that critical skepticism is probably right. Others might resist, refining their vision of rights until they move away from teetering on doctrine's edge between repression and progress, moving until they stand on solid ground. In either case, the choice is made to move forward in the fight against racism in whatever way one can.

Not having all the answers, but having some of them, we dream of stepping over nihilism, as if on air, like the basketball legends of our time.

EPILOGUE: START ACTING YOUR COLOR

At Queen Anne Place Elementary School, in the middle of the Cold War, we were taught the "drop drill." A teacher would yell "drop," and we were to crouch under our desks and wait for a "blinding flash." Don't get up, they said, until the teacher tells you to. I knew that if the blinding flash came, there would be no teacher left to tell us to get up, that our crouching bodies would become shadow imprints on the floor, like the pictures I had seen of the imprints on Hiroshima school yards. Still, I practiced diligently along with my classmates, just in case the teachers were right and there was a chance of surviving. "Keep your chin pressed close to your chest. Put your hands behind the back of your head."

Today, in some urban schools, teachers still do the drop drill, with a difference. The children are taught to lie prone on the ground and close their eyes. This is the bullet drill. The eye-closing is to avoid seeing the blood and torn flesh when drive-by shootings take place just outside the school-yard fence. There are no white children doing the drop drill. The specific form of violence that forces teachers to devise ways to protect their charges from bullets is racially selective.

The generation that grew up doing the Cold War drop drill became the generation that participated in the most significant anti-war movement in American history, the generation that gave such resounding support to nuclear disarmament that politicians had to listen. Who will speak for the current genera-tion of school children, lying on their classroom floors, hoping the teacher's precautions will pay off?

"Stop acting your color," I learned after some asking around, is an admonition of longstanding vintage. Most Black people of a certain age have heard it, sometimes in the variant "act your age and not your color." No doubt the community push to as-similation, to overcompensate for racist stereotypes, to survive by not acting up, kept children alive in the time of lynch law. How will we keep them alive now, when endangered children are kept invisible, when most Americans do not know about the bullet drill, about the boarder babies, about the commonplace of children going to bed hungry in communities of color?

No one else will speak about what no one else sees. From the relative safety of academia, it is time to hear our own voices, to silence the ones that say "stop acting your color." This is the privilege we earned from generations before who made wise choices. They survived so we could flourish, so we could speak up, act up, do right, with our colors flying.

First Annual Workshop on New Developments in Critical Race Theory.

1   Derrick Bell, "The Civil Rights Chronicles," *Harvard Law Review* 99 (1985): 4.

2   Charles Lawrence, "The Word and the River: Pedagogy as Scholarship as Struggle," *Southern California Law Review* 65 (1992): 2231.

3   Critical Legal Studies was a loosely organized group of leftist legal scholars. Key claims in their work included the bankruptcy of liberal legal traditions and the disutility of relying on the purportedly neutral, rule-of-law tradition in seeking radical social change. See Mark Kelman, *A Guide to Critical Legal Studies* (Cambridge: Harvard University Press, 1987) (a survey of the ideas emanating from critical legal studies).

4   See, e.g., Alan Freeman, "Racism, Rights and the Quest for Equality of Opportunity: A Critical Legal Essay," *Harvard Civil Rights–Civil Liberties Law Review* 23 (1988): 295.

5   Charles R. Lawrence III, "The Id, the Ego and Equal Protection: Reckoning with Unconscious Racism," *Stanford Law Review* 39 (January 1987): 317 (explaining the concept of unconscious racism).

6   Kimberlé Williams Crenshaw, "Race, Reform, and Retrenchment: Transformation and Legitimation in Antidiscrimination Law," *Harvard Law Review* 101 (1988): 1331.

7

In 1990, a group of students in my feminist legal theory class at Stanford Law School organized the Third National Conference on Women of Color and the Law. Planning the conference was their research project, undertaken in lieu of the final exam. The work, conflict, elation, and pain that constitute political organizing became a part of these students' lives. Their multicultural alliance inspired me to put into words a political theory emerging from activist coalitions: a theory of the interconnection of all forms of subordination. This theory has many origins—from the 100-year-old multiracial labor movement exemplified by the IWW's "one big union" slogan, to the student movements of the 1960s to 1970s, to the work of lesbian/feminist organizers like Suzanne Pharr who link homophobia with race, gender, and class oppression. It seems that anyone who sits down to think long and hard about the circumstances of her own oppression inevitably looks up to see others with whom to form common cause. This common cause is more than a simple alliance. It is also theory: a means of understanding and moving the world. The following piece was written as a foreword to a collection of papers delivered at the conference, which were published in the Stanford Law Review.[1]

INTRODUCTION

The Stanford Conference on Women of Color and the Law was coalition: individuals from different social positions coming together to work toward a common goal.

The conference possessed the physicality of coalition. From all corners of the country, hundreds of women, and dozens of men, came. They were law students, but their divergences in size, shape, hair, color, speech, and attire were so wondrously dramatic that no outsider who wandered into the large auditorium where they gathered would have thought, "Ah, a meeting of law students." No, it looked more like a gathering of proud tribes. As the participants sat in the sun on perfect Stanford lawns, sipping freshly brewed coffee, they laughed and talked theory as though they did this every weekend. White with Black, native with immigrant, lesbian with straight, teacher with student, women with men—as though the joy of communing across difference was their birthright.

Conference organizers buzzed about busily in their official T-shirts, arranging rides, watching the clock, shepherding speakers, and smoothing over misunderstandings. The organizers and volunteers were as diverse as the audience. White men who looked like they had just wandered over from fraternity row worked alongside their African-Asian-Latina colleagues. Watching these students work so easily with one another made me almost forget that a year of struggle, anger, tears, fears, and consciousness raising had brought them to their day in the sun. Each one had asked, at some point during that long year of working toward the conference, "Is it worth it?" Bernice Johnson Reagan, in her well-known essay on coalition, said, "You don't go into coalition because you just like it." She goes on to state, "And you shouldn't look for comfort. Some people will come to a coalition, and they rate the success of the coalition on whether or not they feel good when they get there. They're not looking for a coalition: they're looking for a home!"[2]

Through our sometimes painful work in coalition, we are beginning to form a theory of subordination. A theory that describes it, explains it, and gives us the tools to end it. As lawyers working in coalition, we develop a theory of law taking sides rather than law as value neutral. We imagine law to uplift and protect the sixteen-year-old single mother on crack rather than law to criminalize her.[3] We imagine law to celebrate and protect women's bodies; law to sanctify love between human beings, whether women to women, men to men, or women to men, as lovers may choose to love; law to respect the bones of our ancestors;[4] law to feed the children; law to shut down the sweat-sweat-shops; and law to save the planet.

This is the revolutionary theory of law that we are developing in coalition, and I submit that this is the theory of law we can develop *only* in coalition and that it is the *only* theory of law we can develop in coalition.

Looking at Subordination from Inside Coalition

When we work in coalition, we compare our struggles and challenge one another's assumptions. We learn a few tentative, starting truths – the building blocks of a theory of subordination.

We learn that all forms of oppression are not the same.[5] We learn about our ignorances and of the gaps and absences in our knowledge. We learn that although all forms of oppression are not the same, certain predictable patterns emerge:

- All forms of oppression involve taking a trait, *x,* often with attached cultural meaning,[6] and using *x* to make some group the other, reducing their entitlements and powers.
- All forms of oppression benefit someone, and sometimes both sides of a relationship of domination have some stake in its maintenance.[7]
- All forms of oppression have both material and ideological dimensions. Subordination leaves marks on the body. It is real. It is material; it is health, economy, and violence. Subordination is also ideology: language – including the language of science and law, rights, necessity, the market, neutrality, and objectivity – can serve to make domination seem natural and inevitable.
- In coalition we learn as well that there is a psychology to subordination, involving elements of sexual fear, need for control, self-hate, and other-hate.
- Finally, and most important, we learn in coalition that all forms of subordination are interlocking and mutually reinforcing, even as they are different and incommensurable.

Ask the Other Question: The Interconnection of All Forms of Subordination

The way I try to understand the interconnection of all forms of subordination is through a method I call "ask the other question." When I see something that looks racist, I ask, "Where is the patriarchy in this?" When I see something that looks sexist, I ask, "Where is the heterosexism in this?" When I see something that looks homophobic, I ask, "Where are the class interests in this?" Working in coalition forces us to look for both the obvious and the nonobvious relationships of domination, and, as we have done this, we have come to see that no form of subordination ever stands alone.[8]

If this is true, we have asked each other, then is it not also true that dismantling any one is impossible without dismantling every other? More and more, particularly in the women-of-color movement, the answer is, "No person is free until the last and the least of us is free."

In trying to explain this in my own community, I sometimes try to shake people up by suggesting that patriarchy killed Vincent Chin. Most people think racism killed Vincent Chin.[9] When white men with baseball bats, hurling racist hate speech, beat a man to death, it is obvious that racism is a cause. It is only slightly less obvious, however, when you walk down the aisles of Toys-R-Us, that little boys grow up in this culture with toys that teach dominance and aggression, while little girls grow up with toys that teach about being pretty, baking, and changing a diaper. The little boy who is interested in learning how to nurture and play house is called a sissy. And when he is a little older he is called f_g.[10] He learns that acceptance for men in this society is premised on rejecting the girl culture and taking on the boy culture, and I believe that this, as much as racism, killed Vincent Chin. I have come to see that homophobia is the disciplinary system that teaches men that they had better talk like 2 Live Crew or else someone will think they "aren't real men," and I believe that this homophobia is a cause of rape and violence against women. I have come to see how that same homophobia makes women scared to choose women and sends them into the arms of men who beat them. I have come to see that class oppression has the same effect, cutting off the chance of economic independence that could free women from dependency on abusive men.

I have come to see all this from working in coalition; from my lesbian colleagues who have pointed out homophobia in places where I failed to see it; from my Native American colleagues who have said, "But remember that we were here first," when I worked for the rights of immigrant women; and from men of color who have risked my wrath to say, "But racism *is* what is killing us, why can't I put that first on my agenda?" The women-of-color movement has, of necessity, been a movement about intersecting structures of subordination. This movement suggests that antipatriarchal struggle is linked to struggle against all forms for subordination.

Beyond Race Alone

What does this mean? In coalition, we develop several levels of understanding that the phenomenon that Professor Crenshaw has called "intersectionality."[11] The women-of-color movement has demanded that the civil rights struggle move beyond race alone, suggesting several reasons why our coalitions must include more than antiracism. These reasons include the following:

1. In unity there is strength. No subordinated group is strong enough to fight the power alone; thus coalitions are formed out of necessity.[12]

2. Some of us have overlapping identity. Separating out and ranking oppression excludes some of these identities

and denies the necessary concerns of significant numbers of our constituency. To say that antiracist struggle proceeds all other struggle denies the existence and needs of the multiply oppressed: women-of-color, gays and lesbians of color, poor people of color, and *most* people of color experience subordination in more than one dimension.

3. Perhaps the most progressive reason for moving beyond race alone is that racism is best understood and struggled against with knowledge gained through comparative study. Even if one wanted to live as the old prototype "race man," it is simply not possible to struggle against racism alone and ever hope to end racism.

This is a threatening suggestion for many of us who have worked primarily in organizations forged in the struggle for racial justice. Our political strength and our cultural self-worth is often grounded in racial pride. Our multiracial coalitions have, in the past, succeeded because of a unifying commitment to end racist attacks on people of color. Moving beyond race, to include discussion of other forms of subordination, risks breaking coalition. Because I believe that the most progressive elements of any liberation movement are those who see the intersections and that the most regressive are those who insist on only one axis, I am willing to risk breaking coalition by pushing intersectional analysis.

An additional and more serious risk, I think, is that an intersectional analysis done from on high, that is, from outside rather than inside a structure of subordination, risks misunderstanding the particularity of that structure. Feminists have spent years talking about, experiencing, and building theory around gender.

Native Americans have spent years developing an understanding of colonialism and its effect on culture. That kind of situated, ground-up knowledge is irreplaceable, and a casual effort to say, "OK, I'll add gender to my analysis," without immersion in feminist practice is likely to miss something. Adding on gender must involve active feminists, just as adding on considerations of indigenous peoples must include activists from Native communities. Coalition is the way to achieve this inclusion.

It is no accident that women-of-color, grounded as they are in both feminist and antiracist struggle, are doing the most exciting theoretical work on race-gender intersections. It is no accident that gay and lesbian scholars are advancing the analysis of sexuality in subordination. In raising this I do not mean that we cannot speak of subordination from the second hand. I mean to encourage us to do this and to suggest we can do this most intelligently in coalition, listening with special care to those who are actively involved in knowing and ending the systems of domination that touch their lives.[13]

CONCLUSION

This essay has suggested a theory of subordination that comes out of work in coalition. The Women-of-Color and the Law Conference is a place for this work. The women and men of many races who worked on the conference can tell us that making this place is not easy. The false efficiencies of law schools, where we edit facts out of cases and cabin concepts such as "crime" and "property" into semester-sized courses, ill-prepare us for the long, slow, open-ended efficiencies of coalition. Planning the conference involved more than inviting speakers and sending out registration forms. It took literally a thousand human hours talking long into the night, telling stories of self and culture and history, before the Stanford Women of Color and the Law Conference could happen. To lay the foundation of trust on which people could teach, challenge, listen, learn, and form theory out of coalition took time and patience. As often happens in the slow-cooking school of theory building, the organizers wondered whether all that talk was getting anywhere. Cutting off discussion and avoiding conflict would have saved hours early on, but coalition at its best never works that way. The slow and difficult early work gives us efficiencies when we need them: when the real challenges come, when justice requires action, and when there is no time to argue over how to proceed. The organizers of the conference have forged bonds and created theory that will sustain them in the contentious closing days of this century. When called on, they will answer with a courage and wisdom born in their place of coalition.

Third National Conference on Women of Color and the Law, Stanford Law School, 1990.

The title of this chapter was inspired by a line from Pablo Neruda, "La Carta en el Camino," *Neruda, Los Versos del Capitan'* (The Captain's Verses) (New York: New Directions, 1972):

> y en medio de la vida estare'
> siempre,
> junto al amigo, frente al enemigo.
> (and in the midst of life I shall be
> always beside the friend, facing the enemy)

1   Papers presented at the conference are compiled in *Stanford Law Review* 43, no. 6 (July 1991). Included are Mari J. Matsuda, "Beside My Sister, Facing the Enemy: Legal Theory Out of Coalition"; Evelyn Nakano Glenn, "Cleaning up/Kept down: A Historical Perspective on Racial Inequality in 'women's work'"; Haunani-Kay Trask, "Coalition-Building

between Natives and non-Natives"; Angela Y. Davis, Keynote address; Kimberlé Crenshaw, "Mapping the Margins: Intersectionality, Identity Politics, and Violence against Women of Color"; Nilda Rimonte, "A Question of Culture: Cultural Approval of Violence against Women in the Pacific-Asian Community and the Cultural Defense"; Patricia Williams, "Reordering Western Civ."; Sharon Parker, "Understanding Coalition"; Chezia Carraway, "Violence against Women of Color"; Judy Scales-Trent, "Women of Color and Health"; and June K. Inuzuka, "Women of Color and Public Policy: A Case Study of the Women's Business Ownership Act."

2   Bernice Johnson Reagan, "Coalition Politics: Turning the Century," in Barbara Smith, *Home Girls, A Black Feminist Anthology* (New York: Kitchen Table – Women of Color Press, 1983), 356. As Professor Kimberlé Crenshaw pointed out, on reading this essay, "Comfort means perfect peace or perfect oppression."

3   See Roberts, "Punishing Drug Addicts Who Have Babies: Women of Color, Equality, and the Right of Privacy," *Harvard Law Review* 104 (1991): 1419.

4   See a conference workshop on burial/remains discussed this issue.

5   See Trina Grillo and Stephanie Wildman, "Obscuring the Importance of Race: The Implication of Making Comparisons between Racism and Sexism (or other isms)," *Duke Law Journal* (1991): 397.

6   See Charles Lawrence, "The Id, the Ego, and Equal Protection: Reckoning with Unconscious Racism," *Stanford Law Review* 39 (1987): 317.

7   For a related discussion of Hegel's theory of the master and slave relationship, see Kendall Thomas, "A House Divided against Itself: A Comment on Mastery, Slavery, and Emancipation," *Cardozo Law Review* 10 (1989): 1481.

8   For an analysis of the relationship between sexism and heterosexism, see, e.g., Suzanne Pharr, *Homophobia: A Weapon of Sexism* (Inverness, Calif.: Chardon Press, 1988).

9   In April of 1989, mine workers in Virginia, West Virginia, and eastern Kentucky went on strike to protest Pittston Coal Company's unfair labor practices regarding health-care benefits for employees. They used Dr. King's technique of non-violent civil disobedience. For a history of the Vincent Chin murder and other cases of anti-Asian violence, see National Asian Pacific American Legal Consortium, *Audit of Violence against Asian Pacific Americans* (1994), which cited 452 reported incidents of anti-Asian

violence in 1994 and noted a severe increase in anti-immigrant sentiment and widespread underreporting of anti-Asian incidents.

10 Throughout this book, homophobic, racist, and mysogynist assault words are altered to omit the vowels. This is an awkward usage that attempts to recognize that these words carry significant social power in our culture and can assault even when used as examples and without intent to harm.

11 See Kimberlé Crenshaw, "Demarginalizing the Intersection of Race and Sex: A Black Feminist Critique of Antidiscrimination Doctrine," *Chicago Legal Forum* (1989): 159.

12 In addition to the political power that comes from unity, there is also a joy and empowerment that comes from finding connections to others. One participant in the Stanford conference noted "the energy that comes from comparing experiences and connecting with others; the nods of 'uh-huh' when one person's story of oppression at one axis triggers another person to remember subordination at a different axis; the making of new friends, the renewal of old friendships; the knowledge that we are not alone in our struggles" are all benefits of coalition work (memo from Tony West, 19 April 1991)

13 See Mari Matsuda, "Pragmatism Modified and the False Consciousness Problem," *Southern California Law Review* 63 (1990): 1763. This piece argues for expanding pragmatic method to account for the intuitions of subordinated people. It responds to false consciousness and essentialism critiques by explaining why the charge to consider the experience of the subordinated is not the equivalent of claiming that all subordinated people are the same or that subordinated status is a necessary prerequisite to understanding subordinated status. That this kind of explanation is necessary in the present world of legal theory is itself evidence of the need for theory building in coalition.

8

*My mother took her babies on the picket line before they could walk, per-
haps because she took seriously the civics lessons she learned as a barefoot
plantation girl in Makawele Kauai. For her, democracy includes a
covenant with citizens to participate actively in self-governance. From in-
fancy to comfortable middle age I have marched with her, and this is the
genesis of the following words on the subject of protest, on the occasion of
the twenty-fifth anniversary of* Brown v. Board of Education.[1]

I stand before you as a person who would not be here but for
social protest in the United States. The opportunities available
to me in education and employment; the privileged status of
law professor – these were not given to me out of the kindness
of the institutions that had for centuries denied entry to women
and people of color. These opportunities were claimed for me
by my mothers and fathers, my sisters and brothers,

> who sat in
> who carried signs
> who walked the long marches
> who rode the freedom rides

who went door-to-door
who dished out food at fundraisers
who stuck stamps on envelopes
who sang freedom songs
who put their bodies on the line for civil rights.

In April 1988, law students across the country held a national day of protest. They sat in to demand changes in hiring practices that to this day keep women, people of color, and gays and lesbians out of legal education. That same year, I got a call inviting me to teach as a visitor at Stanford Law School. In an earlier time, Professor Kimberlé Crenshaw helped organize a student protest movement at Harvard Law School. That protest, which achieved national recognition the year before I entered law teaching, contributed in a real way to my ability to teach, to write about race, and to take a place in legal academia.

The changes in the material lives of excluded citizens that protest has wrought is the first legacy that I celebrate. But the movement has brought us more. It has changed the dominant culture.

It has given dignity to the lives of
    participants
It has focused organizing and coalition building
It has taught, and
It has built theory

It has done this by exploiting cracks and contradictions, by consciously creating, as Dr. King stated time and again, a moment of creative tension in which change could occur. Programmatic struggle against racism pitted the state, with its guns and attack dogs and firehoses, against schoolchildren. The graphic display of repressive force, in response to claims for fair and equal treatment, made clear the choices:

> Side with racism and repression at the risk
>   of your own soul
>   – or –
> Do the right thing.
> Side with the Constitution.
> Side with the best expression of our
>   national ideals.
> Side with those who protest on behalf
>   of human needs.

That was the moral choice presented by those who marched with Ghandi, with Fannie Lou Hammer, with Cesar Chavez and Delores Huerta.[2]

In focusing only on the material changes attained and, particularly obvious today, the material changes *not* attained, we fail to acknowledge the ways in which the civil rights movement dignified its participants by giving them a forum for resistance. In addition to moving the dominant culture toward its more progressive ideals, protest movements claimed human dignity for participants. After years of stoic silence, of backing down, of enduring the daily insult of name-calling, of Jim Crow, and of second-class citizenship, the civil rights movement offered a chance to claim one's personhood.

Understanding this is part of understanding how social change movements can occur even when people are *not* living in a state of utter desperation. Why would a middle-class African-American who has a good job, who has a position of relative privilege, risk all to join the Selma voting-rights drive? Why would a middle-class Japanese-American who already owns a home, who does not *want* to move into an all-white neighborhood, join the Los Angeles campaign against racially restrictive covenants? Why would anyone leave the safety of their living room to go get arrested on the courthouse steps?

Recently, I recalled an event that my younger brother confirms but that my parents do not remember. We were dressed up in our best clothes and about to go on a motorcade to honor a man who died in the civil rights struggle. In retracing the probable time, this would have been the death of Medger Evers, and I was seven years old. As we drove away from the house, my parents explained that if they yelled at us to get down, we were to dive to the floor of the car and stay there until they said to get up.

I think my brother and I were startled, and we remember this because our parents were, to us, cautious people who never let us do anything dangerous, yet here they were driving us off to a place they obviously considered dangerous.

This is not intended as a story of extraordinary sacrifice but as a story of the commonplace. That sunny Sunday, thousands of people got into their cars and drove to memorial services to show they were not afraid, to show they maintained their dignity and citizenship status, to sign up in the army fighting for what seems, in retrospect, a modest victory.

Another image called to mind from this period of struggle is that of middle-class black school teachers going to get arrested while attempting to register to vote. They were wearing suits and good shoes and carrying toothbrushes. The toothbrush was a symbol of their willingness to spend the night in jail.

There is something so bourgeois about that — "I can't go to sleep without brushing my teeth" — and something at once so incredibly courageous. Why did they do it? Knowing they risked life and livelihood in the days when Birmingham was known as Bombingham, with no evidence on the immediate record that they would win. Why was their personal dignity worth so much to them that they would choose the freedom struggle over the instinct of immediate self-preservation?

Of course they wanted the vote, but they wanted also to reclaim their personhood, to say publicly, "We are willing to give up all the privilege you have doled out to us in order to claim our dignity." That kind of determination was a signal to those in power: if you resist this change, you face those who are willing to risk all.

Remembering the ways in which large numbers of middle- and upper-class people of color were drawn into the civil rights movement — not without conflict, but drawn in nonetheless — can tell us something about the human will to freedom. It can save us from the dangerous notion that things have to get very bad before they get better. People need not be starving and bleeding before they rise up and demand decent treatment.

Looking at the history of the civil rights movement, we learn about organizing and coalition making. We can see how patriarchy, homophobia, class divisions, and red-baiting are internal barriers that social change movements must avoid. I am excited to see students in today's protest movements emphasizing multiracial, antipatriarchal strategies in their protests. I am excited to see them engaging in consciousness raising over homophobia, moving to the center voices silenced in the last era of campus mobilization. I am amazed to watch students born *after* the sixties rehashing the SNCC-CORE[3] debates, reading movement history, and attempting to learn from and avoid the mistakes of the past.

Protest, for those involved in it, is always primarily a response to immediate repression, but the pedagogical reverberations of protest rebound in time and space. Those who marched with Ghandi taught those who marched with King. Those who sat in with King taught those who sit in today at the Pittston coal mines.[4]

> They teach that change is possible.
> That change comes only through struggle,
> That structures of domination are real, but not
>   impenetrable,
> That community organizing around immediate
>   needs is an efficient starting place in meeting
>   larger goals of social transformation.

The current debates among intellectuals about whether structural change is possible, about which transformations are truly liberating, about the naivete of hope and the destructiveness of pure deconstruction – these are debates enriched and informed by the study of social protest movements.

We need to do more than study. We need to participate. Students in SNCC were fond of asking, when armchair liberals and intellectuals expressed sympathy for the movement, "Where is your body?" Those of us in U.S. academia, unlike teachers in South Africa, are not called on to put our bodies before assault weapons to protect our students. But we will have to decide, as the great campus protest movement of the 1990s escalates, which side we are on.

The critical pedagogy of protest is bringing us to the eve of the third and last American Reconstruction. It is protest

> over sexual assault of women
> over homelessness
> over plant closings
> over apartheid,
> over environmental and nuclear omnicide
> over cutbacks in financial aid and affirmative action
> over Native American cultural rights
> over homophobia
> over U.S. military adventurism

The theory generated from current protest is a theory of the structural forms of domination and the interrelationships of those structures. We are coming to see how racism relates to armed aggression against third-world democracies; how union busting relates to the spread of toxic chemicals in the environment; how homophobia pushes men to violence to "prove their manhood"; how violence becomes sexualized and entrenches patriarchy; how patriarchy impoverishes women and makes the rich richer; and how the lust for profit maintains militarism, environmental disaster, and homelessness.

I am reminded almost daily of Catharine MacKinnon's admonition that a strategy of formal equality will benefit those who can most closely approximate the biography of the upper-class white man.[5] Although a handful of women of color are now teaching in law schools, the doors are still closed to most, regardless of ability. Outside the universities, growing numbers of my sisters are living in poverty and degradation. I cannot offer thanks and celebration without offering as well a challenge to those of us who have squeaked through the door on the tail of the last civil rights movement.

When the new protest movement rises up from the crisis of poverty, racism, militarism, homophobia, and patriarchy that is tearing apart our communities, will we risk loss of our privilege? Can we remember our debt to those who risked all for us?

When the schoolteachers walked to the courthouse, toothbrushes in hand, they were not thinking of me, an Asian woman who wants to teach law. They are old women now, full of peace, I imagine, knowing as they do that they stood tall in a moment of history making. Wherever they are, I thank them for the world of possibilities they opened and for their gracious example of Constitutional interpretation through protest.

---

1   University of Wisconsin, November 1989.
2   Fannie Lou Hammer was a civil rights activist and co-founder of the Mississippi Freedom Democratic Party, which was formed in response to the racism of the Mississippi Democratic Party; Cesar Chavez was a civil rights activist and co-founder and president of the United Farm Workers, which represented the interests of Chicano migrant workers; and Delores Huerta is co-founder and vice president of the United Farm Workers.
3   Student Nonviolent Coordinating Committee; Congress for Racial Equality.
4   In April of 1989, mine workers in Virginia, West Virginia, and eastern Kentucky went on strike to protest Pittston Coal Company's unfair labor practices regarding health-care benefits for employees. They used Dr. King's technique of non-violent civil disobedience.
5   See Catharine MacKinnon, *Feminism Unmodified: Discourses on Life and Law* (Cambridge: Harvard University Press, 1989).

PART **II**

WHO OWNS SPEECH? *Language and Power*

9

For years I worked separately on the issues of racist hate speech and lin-
guistic discrimination. As the antisubordination analysis in both works
converged, I realized they were in fact one project. The English-only
movement says, "You can only use the words I say you can use,"
whereas the freedom-for-hate-speech argument says, "I am free to ex-
clude you with my words." In both cases a fight about language masks
an effort to dominate and control. Once I came to see fights about lan-
guage in this way, related battles seemed to emerge everywhere. This
chapter was presented as the Library of Congress's Holmes Devise Lec-
ture in Washington, D.C., October 5, 1992.

INTRODUCTION

Who owns speech? A central premise of our liberal notion of
the First Amendment to the U.S. Constitution is that each of us
owns our own speech. We own this speech as a sacred element
of our humanity. It is ours prior to the state, and intervention
with our speech is presumptively beyond state power. The state
cannot tell us what to say. It cannot dictate what we listen to. It
cannot censor the content of our message.

I state this liberal ideal at the outset not because I intend to deconstruct it but because it comprises values I adhere to as a lawyer and as a human being. Those values include promotion of democratic discourse, respect for individual choices, and tolerance of difference. This discussion is intended as part of the search for ways to live out those values and particularly for a notion of the First Amendment that holds fast to those values by recognizing the complexity, contradiction, and confusion built into the liberal notion of free speech.

Like John Stuart Mill, I believe we each own our own expression, but, unlike him, I do not see individual expression as disconnected from the wide social context that gives speech meaning. Speech emanates not from the individual alone but also from the collective. I will discuss several seemingly unrelated topics that I believe reveal the contradiction inherent in a notion of the First Amendment that fails to recognize the social nature of speech.

WHAT IS CONTENT?

Much of this contradiction is evident in the content distinction. In the broadest terms, jurists have attempted to carve out a part of speech that is protected, the substantive content, and to leave unprotected the part that is nonsubstantive, or free of content.[1] This carving out is evident in rules permitting time, place, and manner restrictions.[2] The state cannot limit the content of what you say, but it can limit the way in which you say it. Another application of the content distinction is in the area of commercial speech. Certain speech—"buy this now, lowest prices in town"—is really just commerce; it is not substantive politics.[3] It has low content value, properly subject to more restrictions than high-content speech. Similarly, in obscenity law, courts have attempted to distinguish content-free sex depictions from the content-laden artistic or political messages communicated in sexual art and literature.[4] All these efforts to separate content from noncontent have backed courts into doctrinal corners that law professors and law students have fun pointing out. Are we smarter than the judges? Consider the following case.

A pro-military law student at the University of Minnesota, upset by a campus ban on employers who refuse to sign nondiscrimination statements, formed an organization called the Free Speech Movement.[5] The Free Speech Movement invited military recruiters to come to the law school to give speeches in an attempt to recruit students for the military. The school denied a forum for these speeches, arguing they were simply a subterfuge for getting around the school's antidiscrimination policy. A judge who reviewed the decision to exclude the military recruiter's speeches decided that the purpose of the speech was commerce—an attempt to persuade someone to exchange labor for a price.[6] Because it was commerce, the judge concluded, it was not protected speech.

I believe the school was correct in denying use of campus facilities to employers who discriminate against members of the law school community. The school's action was itself a form of speech, although this was not part of its defense. Although the school's enforcement of the nondiscrimination policy was ethically defensible, the commercial speech exception was not a strong rationale for keeping the military recruiters off campus. Military recruiters do engage in substantive, political speech when they say, "Come work for us; this is a good job, a noble way to spend one's life." In fact, it may be the most substantive speech there is. It is speech exhorting citizens to participate in an ideological system—militarism—that has the potential to kill. That is about as political as it gets.

Was the judge just a weak jurist? Or is there something about the content distinction that makes us weak jurists?

I suggest the latter. The content distinction is impossible to apply with clarity because it ignores a linguistic premise: *all* speech has content. A simple "Good morning" can convey love, harassment, indifference, threat of violence, pleasure, anger, or insanity, depending on the context. This suggests another linguistic premise: the meaning of speech is largely a social meaning. It is dependent on context, culture, and social relations. The function of speech is not simply to communicate the facial information conveyed in the speech. It is also to communicate a social message. Speech positions people socially.[7] Existing First Amendment doctrine fails to account for this.

When the first woman to work in a formerly all-male workplace is asked daily about her sex life,[8] shown pictures of naked women,[9] and told that her private body parts are attractive to men,[10] the facial message is only incidental to the social message: you are someone we feel free to humiliate and demean.[11] You are not welcome here. We do not see you as human. You are not safe here. If you do not quit this job, we will escalate our assault on you.

The idea that the facial information conveyed in speech is often secondary to its social message is recognized in the political world. Concern over such social messages lies behind what I call competition over linguistic space.

COMPETITION OVER LINGUISTIC SPACE

Here is an example. Lawmakers in California and elsewhere are deeply concerned about a new social problem, namely, the proliferation of signs in Asian languages, using Asian characters, primarily Chinese and Korean. In response to the perceived sign problem, a variety of local government officials have proposed ordinances to limit the use of non-English characters on signs in public places.[12] Some of these ordinances outlaw non-English signs altogether.[13] Some, usually in places where Asian-American civil rights groups have intervened, merely require English translations.[14] One community, in the visual enactment of formal equality, proposed that where non-English characters are used, equal square inches must be allotted to English characters.[15] Another took a more bullying approach: foreign characters must remain one-third the size of English characters.[16]

The legislative history of these ordinances is revealing. A city council member in Pomona, in a memo in support of an English-only sign rule, stated, "Because of the liberalization of immigration policies, a heavy influx of Asian/orientals have taken up residence in the United States, many of them in California. Their natural entrepreneurship has directed many of them into business ownership in many California cities, and those cities have been impacted by a proliferation of advertising and signs which consist of oriental characters. That practice has caused dissent and strife in our communities. In order to prevent the introduction of such racial and ethnic strife in our City, it is recommended that the City Council, by ordinance, require all public signs or advertising to be in the English language, permitting only sub-titles or explanatory language to be in foreign characters."[17]

In Monterey Park, one city council member said, "I've talked to a lot of people about this and they want to feel like it's their town, too, not just a Chinese town. Why should

Monterey Park be called the Chinese Beverley Hills?" She added, "It's more than just English only; I want signs that look like we're in America."[18]

Some argue that English signs are necessary on commercial buildings so that those who cannot read Asian languages will know what kind of business is housed within, to which one business owner, Christine Ching, replied, "If city hall guarantees me business from white people, English-speaking people, I'll put a big sign in English out in front."[19] Ching's business is a print shop with specialized equipment that prints in Chinese.

The "if we can't read it, how will we know what they are selling?" argument seems disingenuous in light of the claim that Asians are "natural entrepenuers." For years the fancy suburbs have touted their "high demos," as the ad people call them, with boutiques and restaurants with a host of European names that many patrons could not pronounce correctly, much less translate. In Los Angeles, the ultimate chic is the restaurant with no sign. If you have to ask, you are not invited, I learned one night as I drove back and forth in front of the address of the sushi bar where I was supposed to meet some friends.[20] There was no sign, no facade, just a plain storefront with a heavy door.

Another argument in favor of English-only sign rules is that emergency vehicles will not be able to find a business if it does not have an English sign. This argument weakens when we note the sushi bar without a sign and the general absence of laws requiring any kind of sign at all. Furthermore, if public safety requires more accurate identification, there are certainly better alternatives than a law that forbids Chinese characters. A few municipalities have gotten fire and law enforcement personnel to submit written testimony that it is easier to find buildings when they are called "Joe's Bar and Grill," but when they have not been coached, firefighters have said things like, "That's not how we find burning buildings."

The real reason for the sign ordinances is that taking up linguistic space with writing that looks Asian is deeply offensive to some non-Asians. Signs in Thai, Chinese, or Korean convey the social message of multiculturalism: Asian people are here to stay, they have different languages and cultures, they are proud of that, and they do not see English, or Anglo culture, as the center of life. Fear of this message fuels the English-only movement. Listen to the words of another Monterey Park councilman: "This is America. I pay a good amount of my income on my mortgage. I come home from my job. I get off the freeways. I get away from the maddening world, and I come home. And when I drive downtown, in my little town . . . the signs are all in Chinese. . . . Then you feel like you're not quite home. You feel like an alien, or that you're in a foreign country."[21]

This council member also supports bans on what he calls the "hordes" and "floods" of immigration[22] and opposes the use of library funds for buying "Chinese or other foreign language books."[23] Others testifying in Monterey Park said things like, "Our city has bent over backwards long enough to accommodate our new immigrants. We now say enough is enough." A twenty-year resident argued that buildings in the pagoda style are "grating. . . . This is America and it has no place for architecture like that. The Chinese just aren't conforming, and I resent that."

What is America supposed to look like? There have been Chinese people and Chinese signs in California since the days when Spanish was the predominant language of the Southwest, since way before the so-called longtime residents who complain about Chinese signs were born. There were signs in Hebrew, Russian, Español, Greek, German, and Japanese when my father was a child in Boyle Heights and when I was a child in city-center L.A. Generations of Angelenos have lived with these signs. This is what America looks like. Some have made money from it, packaging and marketing a taste of ethnic diversity in restaurants, tours, and festivals.

The sign ordinances are about who controls linguistic space: who says what, where, and when. It is okay to have Groman's Chinese theater. It is okay to have Chinatown. We will even try Thai food, but we will control when and where we will try on the culture of the other. They should not have control over their choice to practice their linguistic difference in our neighborhood.

Linguistic anxiety is the new proxy for racial anxiety. Jim Crow, restrictive covenants, and burning crosses are now considered socially inappropriate. So the new language of exclusion becomes "Those signs make me feel like it's not America, like I'm excluded. I have nothing against them, but why can't they use English?"

The anxiety in Pomona and Monterey Park is understood only in the historical context of white flight. The subtext of "When I get off the freeway in my little town . . ." is "I moved to the suburbs so I wouldn't have to live next to people who aren't like me."

Even as I criticize it, I try to understand the feeling of displacement and insecurity that prompted the sign ban. I try to understand the student who told me he was enraged when Spanish started appearing at the terminal of the automatic teller machine alongside the English he had become accustomed to. There was this stranger's language, suddenly appearing in a familiar, private space where he communed with the market. I appreciate the honesty of this student. His reaction, which he raised precisely because it troubled him, reflects a cognitive reality that we are socialized to in this society, like it or not. We perceive a world of limited goods and limited space, and this includes linguistic space. If new speech comes into the speech box, then something old and valuable is displaced. There is only so much room in the box. The box metaphor, so hopelessly inappropriate when it comes to language—because languages expand worlds and expand visions—is the one we use because it is an old cognitive habit. If you can speak Chinese here, then there is no room for me and my English. I am no longer the center of things, and being in the center of things is everything in a world that presumes "haves" and "have-nots," some people inside the box and some people outside the box.

This is why we are seeing so many viciously fought battles over linguistic space. Can gay Irish march in the St. Patrick's Day parade? Can discriminatory clubs march in Mardi Gras? Can a Columbus descendant serve as Grand Marshall for the Rose Parade? None of the contestants in these battles considered the decision about who will march a trivial one. The expression of a particular identity in the public and highly symbolic arena of a state-supported parade determines who is in and who is out of the box.

This wearing of the green shamrock *and* the pink triangle in the same space is inconceivable for those who subscribe to the notion of linguistic space as a limited good, owned only by the deserving, the divinely destined, the designated insiders. So a berth in the parade is fought over viciously, as if all one's power and privilege depended on it. In a world where ideology does distribute material goods, including freedom from violence, I recognize these struggles as critical. That is, who marches in the parade is linked to whom we feel it is okay to batter and bash. If you are inside, you are real, an object of empathy. If you are outside, you are neither.

The bitter objection to the presence of someone in a "Gay, Irish, and Proud" T-shirt goes to the social message of that shirt: "I am here. I am out. Don't be so sure about your own or anyone else's sexuality. Heterosexual assumptions are about to crumble." Given this message, the decision about who marches in which parade is not content free. I submit that there is no value-free way to resolve this issue. Before I explain how I would resolve it, let me tell you of another case that captures our confusion over content regulation.

WHAT IS HISTORY?

Librarians, as keepers of a significant linguistic space, are increasingly caught in this crossfire. I have already mentioned the debates over foreign-language books and services to non-English speakers. In a time when libraries across the country are forced to cut hours and services because of gross underfunding, the non-English services are often the first to go. What is the center? What is expendable?

Librarians are also increasingly burdened with the fallout of the collapse of the welfare state: children who have nowhere to go after school and the homeless looking for shelter from the cold. At least one library has argued in court for the right to eject homeless patrons who offend other library users.[24] The homeless, it is said, mumble. They have offensive odors. In a time

when providing shelter and warm baths is not considered anyone's responsibility, courts have upheld the right to exclude the
unbathed.[25]

The insanity of the fight for the largess of librarians, and our
confusion over speech and linguistic space, culminates for me in
a recent case from the Ninth Circuit U.S. Court of Appeals.[26]
The librarians of California were planning their annual meeting,
and a Holocaust denial group asked for space and time to put on
a program at the meeting. I must interrupt stating the case here
to make clear where I stand on this. I believe that there are standards we can apply to the enterprise of historical inquiry and that
no Holocaust hoax claim can meet them. The Holocaust hoax
claim is an assaultive and ugly form of anti-Semitism that deserves no audience among ethical people.

The librarians do not agree. Committed as they apparently
are to versions of free-speech absolutism and relativism that
would protect Holocaust deniers, they agreed to let the program be a part of the annual meeting.[27] Jewish groups in Los
Angeles, where the meeting was planned, immediately informed the librarian's association that if the program went on,
it would be met with vigorous protest. According to the First
Amendment traditionalists, this is exactly what is supposed to
happen. If you do not like the speech, then engage in counterspeech.

But what in fact happened was the Holocaust denial group
brought an action for damages against the Jewish groups on a
variety of what, in my legal opinion, are completely frivolous
claims, including tortious interference with contract and a state
civil rights claim.[28] The Ninth Circuit, in a split opinion, allowed the suit to go forward. The allegation of threats of

demonstrations, including nonspecific claims of predictions of property damage, raised sufficient questions of fact, Judge Norris held for a three-judge panel. The court split again in an opinion deciding not to reconsider the case en banc – before the entire court. One interesting thing about that opinion, in addition to the important legal issues it raises, is that you could not predict where the judges would come out based on their politics.

Judge Kozinsky, a conservative, was joined by Judge Reinhardt, a liberal, in expressing the dissenting side.[29] He argued that mere allegations that demonstrations threatened the plaintiff were insufficient given the competing speech interest of the demonstrators. Citing a "hall of fame" of civil rights cases, including *New York Times v. Sullivan*,[30] he noted that lawsuits against protesters have a chilling effect on critically important political expression. The courts have a special responsibility to dismiss lawsuits designed to chill speech.[31]

Parts of Kozinsky's opinion read like critical race theory in that he evoked the images of Kristallnacht, of frozen boxcars, and of Dachau to explain the historical context of the protests.[32] He used passion and real life experience, considering, as critical race theorists have urged judges to do, the ways in which anti-Semitic speech assaults targets. He concluded that if threats of protest from Holocaust survivors take on hot language, that must be understood in context.

Although Judge Kozinsky and I are in agreement there, my reading of the opinion is that he would reject my position that the holocaust hoax group does not deserve a forum. Both Kozinsky and Reinhardt seem to believe that the anti-Semitic revisionists have a right to speak to the librarians, as do the protesters. Let them all speak.

This is the classic liberal response. I have pointed out elsewhere that we do not protect speech that hurts property or reputation interests, but somehow when speech targets women, Jews, gays, or people of color for assault, this is seen as "political" and therefore protected.[33] I have asked that we reconsider this position because assaultive speech seriously infringes on liberty, equality, and speech interests of target groups.[34]

In the hate-speech debate, in the sexual harassment debate, and in the so-called PC debate, I see continued confusion and conflict over the linguistic space of the academy. I have heard the same professors argue that we cannot restrict hate speech because it is political, it is the price of liberty, and then turn around and argue that a student who objects to sexist comments in the classroom is "censoring" the professor, enforcing a PC orthodoxy. On the one hand, the market is seen as working: hate speech, pornography, homophobic speech, Holocaust hoax claims — let them all flourish, and let us criticize them. On the other hand, when new voices come to the academy and challenge traditional methodologies, object to stereotyping, and get hot about institutional racism, the market is seen as collapsed. Collegiality, culture, and canon are all at risk, awash in a sea of special interest, coercion, market distortion, and bias.

"F_gg_t, I hope you die of AIDS," shouted out by a law student last year at Stanford, encompassed an idea of homophobia.[35] It also functioned as an assault. It was intended as an assault by the speaker, and it was experienced as one by the target, the same as spitting in the face. Students have told me that they avoid places where they know they will encounter this kind of speech; that they fear speaking out on gay-rights issues because of the kind of verbal and physical abuse that often follows.[36] We do our students and colleagues no favors when we glorify abusive disregard for other human beings by wrapping it in the First Amendment.[37] Somewhere along the road to protecting speech, we have conveyed the message that it is okay to speak with the intent of silencing, wounding, degrading, excluding, and cutting another person to their core, that this is good for democracy and for intellectual discourse. We have concluded that offensive body odors are grounds for exclusion but that racist slurs are not, that Holocaust hoax tracts are plausible scholarship, whereas protests against them are violations of civil rights.

Whether or not you agree with my particular doctrinal reconstruction of the First Amendment, let me suggest that our thinking about free speech has to get beyond the false comfort of formalism. By formalism I mean easy categories generating easy answers — as in "It is political, therefore it is protected"; and "It is commercial, therefore it is not protected"; and "Homophobia is an idea, Holocaust revisionism is history, snuff porn is art" — as though calling something "idea" or "history" or "art" ends the analysis and ends all responsibility for evaluating the impact of speech on our lives and our bodies.

BEYOND THE CONTENT DISTINCTION

What history has given us is speech — linguistic space — as a playing ground on which we struggle over power and ascendancy. Our contests over speech, over what is permissible in the communities we make — our workplaces, our schools, our scholarly meetings — both reflect and make the harm that is possible to human beings.

My goal is to rethink the First Amendment and the concept of free speech in a way that acknowledges this. Rather than relying on the content distinction to throw us into either absolute protection of speech or absolute censorship, we need to talk about ways to distinguish among the different kinds of content. We need to do the hard work of delineating a distinction between dissent and assault and between tolerance of difference and tolerance of subordination. In supporting those who would protest the Holocaust hoax, Judge Reinhardt recalled the NAACP, the IWW, and the Vietnam War protesters.[38] These groups were challenging the most powerful institutions of their times. Speaking against power is not the same as speaking against the powerless. I call for a recognition that the first core of the First Amendment is dissent: the inalienable right of the people to speak out against the conditions that oppress them.

The second core is tolerance: the notion that there is no enforced center in belief, in culture or in religion, in this country. Respecting differences is tied to our survival. I say this in an age in which war and violence happen daily because of hatred of difference. To meet this very goal of tolerance, we need to identify the times when tolerance of intolerance has the effect of reinforcing the forms of subordination the Bill of Rights struggles against. Signs in Chinese or Korean hurt no one. The fear of these signs is explainable only by the ideology of yellow peril, the same ideology that landed my father's family behind barbed wire fifty years ago today. Tolerance of signs in Asian characters, enforced by law, creates the counterideology that is the public overruling of the *Korematsu* case.[39] We need to do this, for we are all, always, in this scary world, at risk of barbed wire enclosures.

Tolerance of gay bashing, Holocaust deniers, and burning crosses is not the same. It is only the same if we are innocent of history, if we live in some world where bodies are crushed at random, and not according to ideologies of domination. The tolerance principle dissolves into absurdity unless it is adjunct to the antisubordination principle.[40] This is why I would grant to parade organizers any choices in culture and difference they choose, except the choice to subordinate. I define subordination contextually so that the exclusion of gays must be understood in light of the history of homophobia and violence against gays. The Holocaust hoax tracts must be understood in light of the history of anti-Semitism and genocide against Jews.

In arguing for this contextualized interpretation, I am told the task is impossible. We cannot draw those lines and cannot know history with the certainty required for legal analysis. I do not see how we can do anything else. The know-nothingness of pure tolerance is an inadequate response in a world of growing violence and, in my view, does not achieve freedom.

In questioning the content distinction, I do not mean to discard the commitment to free exchange of ideas that the distinction represents. Rather, I intend to complexify our discussions about content to include recognition of both sociolinguistic reality and the material reality of the harm and exclusion that flows from some of what we now consider protected speech.

To do this is both easier and harder than formalism—easier because, as Justice Holmes noted long ago, defending unworkable distinctions ultimately makes tired fools out of eager jurists and harder because attention to power relations, to the functioning of democracy, to the connection between speech and violence, and to social meanings is hard work and largely foreign to the discipline of jurisprudence. As I learn from feminist practitioners staffing the shelters, from gay activists monitoring violence, from social historians uncovering forgotten parts of our past, and from sociolinguists mapping the real world of speech, I remain convinced that we can do it. We can devise a rule of law that encompasses what we now know about the complexity of social life.

The question opening this lecture was, Who owns speech? Those who see the space for speech as paltry and hard will continue grabbing desperately for control of that space, often using speech as a weapon of assault. Those who see speech as beyond owning will know the gift of its infinite space, turning ownership metaphors around, as Professor Patricia Williams has said, until a precious, golden spirit owns us.[41]

---

1   See, e.g., *Gertz v. United States*, 418 U.S. 323, 339–40 ("Under the First Amendment there is no such thing as a false idea. However pernicious an opinion may seem, we depend for its correction not on the conscience of judges and juries but on the competition of other ideas.").

2   See, e.g., *United States v. Grace*, 461 U.S. 171, 177 (1983) ("[T]he government may enforce reasonable time, place and manner regulations as long as the restrictions 'are content-neutral, are narrowly tailored to serve a significant government interest, and leave open ample channels of communication,'" quoting *Perry Education Association v. Perry Local Educator's Assn.*, 460 U.S. 37, 45 (1983)).

3   See *Bolger v. Young's Drug Products Corp.*, 463 U.S. 60, 64 (1975) ("[T]his court extended the protection of the First Amendment to commercial speech. Nonetheless, our decisions have recognized the 'common-sense' distinction between speech proposing a commercial transaction, which occurs in an area traditionally subject to government regulation, and other varieties of speech."). See also *Central Hudson Gas & Electric Corp. v. Public Service Commission of New York*, 447 U.S. 5557 (1980), and *Virginia Pharmacy Board v. Virginia Citizens Consumer Council, Inc.*, 425 U.S. 748 (1976).

4   *Pope v. Illinois*, 481 U.S. 497, 500 (1987) ("In Miller itself, the Court was careful to point out that 'the First Amendment protects works which, taken as a whole, have serious literary, artistic, political, or scientific value, regardless of whether the government or a majority of the people

approve of the ideas these works represent,' " citing *Miller v. California,*
413 U.S. 15, 34 [1973].). See also, *FCC v. Pacifica,* 438 U.S. 726 (1978)
("Some uses of even the most offensive words are unquestionably protected.").

5   *Nomi v. Regents for the University of Minnesota,* 796 F. Supp. 412 (D. Minn.
1992). (Vacated as moot, 5 F. 3d 332 [8th Civ. 1993].

6   Ibid., at 417. ("[T]he purpose of recruiting is to reach an agreement under
which services will be exchanged for compensation. The fact that the
military, rather than a civilian employer, initiates the transaction does not
alter its essential [commercial] nature.)

7   See William Labov, *Sociological Patterns* (Philadelphia:University of Pennsylvania Press, 1978); and John J. Gumperz, ed., *Language and Social Identity* (Cambridge: Cambridge University Press, 1988).

8   See *Henson v. City of Dundee,* 682 F. 2d 897 (1982) (Plaintiff claimed that
the defendant subjected her and her co-worker to "numerous harangues
of demeaning sexual inquiries".).

9   *Robinson v. Jacksonville Shipyards,* 760 F. Supp. 1486 (1991) (Plaintiff asserted that the presence in the workplace of pictures of women in various
stage of undress and in sexually suggestive or submissive poses created a
sexually hostile work environment.).

10 *Rabidue v. Osceola Refining Co.,* 584 F. Supp. 419 (1984) (Plaintiff asserted
that the defendant used vulgar language around the office, making ob-
scene comments about women's private body parts.).

11 Catharine MacKinnon, *Feminism Unmodified* (Cambridge: Harvard University Press, 1989), 107. See generally Catharine MacKinnon, *Sexual Harassment of Working Women: A Case of Sex Discrimination* (New Haven: Yale
University Press, 1979) (analyzing the coercive effect of sexual harassment).

12 See note 15 below.

13 Temple City (California) Ordinance, no. 85-577 (restricting five-block
downtown commercial area to English only. Council members argued
that a mix of English and Chinese characters would create a "garish" appearance [*Los Angeles Times,* 30 April 1985, Metro 2]).

14 Mike Ward, "Chinese Only? Monterey Park Sees the Signs," Los Angeles
Times, 30 April 1985, 1.

15 Pomona City Ordinance, sec. 3–7, no. 3467. Similar English-only sign
ordinances have been passed in states on the East Coast, including New
Jersey and Georgia. See, e.g., Paul Toomey, "7 Towns' English Sign Laws
Attacked," *The Record,* 24 April 1996, p.A1; and Tim Fay, "English-only

Bill Dominates International Press," *The Atlanta Journal and Constitution,* 16 February 1995, p. A7.

16 Arcadia City Ordinance, sec. 9262.4.15, 9262.4.18.

17 Clay Bryant, "Public Advertising, Language Requirement," *The City of Pomona Memorandum,* 18 October 1988.

18 Hudson, "Monterey Park Grapples Anew with Language Law," *Los Angeles Times* (San Gabriel Section), 15 September 1988, 1.1.

19 Ibid.

20 The name of the restaurant is Katsu.

21 See note 18 above.

22 Ibid.

23 Ibid.

24 *Kreimer v. Morristown,* 958 F. 2d 1242 (3rd Cir.1992).

25 Ibid. See also Robert Hanley, "Library Wins in the Homeless-Man Case," *New York Times,* 25 March 1992, A14.

26 *McCalden v. California Library Assn.,* 955 F. 2d 1214 (9th Cir. 1992).

27 Ibid., at 1217.

28 Ibid.

29 Ibid. at 1227.

30 376 U.S. 254 (1964).

31 *McCalden,* at 1227.

32 Ibid., at 1230.

33 Mari Matsuda et al., *Words That Wound* (Boulder, Colo.: Westview Press, 1993).

34 Ibid.

35 Jeff Gottlieb, "Campus Anti-Gay Incident Unites Law School in Anger," *San Jose Mercury News.*

36 See, e.g., student testimony before the Senate Labor and Human Resources Committee on S.1484, 19 September 1992.

37 See, e.g., Alan Dershowitz, "Harvard Witch Hunt Burns the Incorrect at the Stake," *Los Angeles Times,* 22 April 1992, B7.

38 *McCalden,* at 1228–34.

39 *Korematsu v. United States,* 319 U.S. 432 (1943).

40 For a fuller discussion of this argument, see Matsuda, et al., *Words That Wound.*

41 Patricia Williams, *The Alchemy of Race and Rights* (Cambridge: Harvard University Press, 1990).

10

The debate over assaultive speech and the First Amendment is covered in depth in an earlier book, Words That Wound, *which I co-authored with three fellow critical race theorists. This speech, which I gave at several universities that were in the midst of speech code debates, applies the thesis of* Words That Wound *in the context of the debate over campus speech codes and academic freedom.*

Ten years ago I began speaking to university and community groups about sexual harassment. An eerie pattern emerged in these speaking forays. After I would give my talk about the legal analysis of sexual harassment, throwing in a little bit of feminist theory and answering a predictable array of questions about what is and what is not sexual harassment, I would conclude and prepare to leave. The crowd would thin out, and a woman would remain on its edges, waiting to talk to me. When she was certain the others were out of hearing range, she would come up to me and say, in a voice both guilty and grateful for the chance to speak, "It happened to me." Secretaries told me of bosses who chased them around desks, men they were afraid to be in elevators with, and jobs they had to leave because "he

couldn't keep his hands off me." Students told me of professors
who would call them into the office for special conferences that
turned out to be sexual propositions. I heard these stories regularly about downtown law firms and college campuses. Suddenly
the elegant offices and the broad, tree-lined walkways of the universities looked different because, underneath the appearance of
normalcy, I came to see an epidemic of hateful behavior toward
women. Students would call me anonymously to tell me stories
rich with the kind of detail that comes from the truth. A thera-
pist wrote to tell me she believed a patient of hers was date-raped
by a professor. I learned the techniques of the academic ha-
rasser – how particularly adept some of them are at exploiting the
student's wishes for more intimate contact in a large university
and how the antihierarchy of the counterculture is used to con-
fuse students about the limits of appropriate intimacy in academic relationships.

As I heard these stories, as I heard from women who had left
school, who had changed majors, who had gone into therapy,
and who blamed themselves for the aggression of others, I perceived an emergency, appropriately responded to by regulations against sexual harassment. To my surprise, many of my
colleagues disagreed. Rules against sexual harassment, particularly rules against so-called voluntary sexual relations between
students and faculty, were seen as violations of academic freedom and personal choice. Women have to toughen up, I was
told. They need to stop thinking like victims and learn to stand
up to harassers. Regulations against harassment could lead to a
chilling effect, preventing warm student-teacher relations.
Proposals for regulation were antisex, antilove, and authori-
tarian.

In the meantime, I was also researching and writing on the topic of assaultive racist speech and traveling to various universities making legal arguments that are viewed as heresy by many civil libertarians – not all civil libertarians, I would add, for I myself am a member of the ACLU. I argued that racist speech is appropriately regulated because of its impact on victims. At every single university at which I spoke – north, south, east, and west – I learned of serious incidents of racist, homophobic, or anti-Semitic hate. University administrators reported that they had never seen anything like it. A pattern emerged in the 1980s of the new integration colliding with the new racism – or the new old racism. The universities, long the home of institutional and euphemistic racism, were now seeing something different: the worst forms of gutter racism. Asian-American students spat on; Nazi literature appearing on Jewish holy days; and cross burnings, racist slurs, and homophobic insults so degrading and assaultive that I found I could not in good conscience reprint them, even for educational purposes, in the book I wrote on the topic.

When university administrators were faced with these horrific incidents, they were understandably shocked and dismayed. Often the incidents were attributed to outsiders, but increasingly the facts – for example, hate messages delivered to the mailboxes of African-American students when only someone who knew who was who on campus could pick the right boxes – pointed to our own students. The response to the crisis was mixed. Some universities immediately sought to find and punish the perpetrators. Others chose to do nothing on the grounds of free speech and due process.

When a few scholars and advocates began to call for campus regulations directed at hate speech, a wave of protest came forth.

We cannot punish speech. Academic freedom requires that people remain free to say what they please at a university.[1]

What I have seen in both the racist speech debate and the sexual harassment debate is an emerging thematic conflict going to the heart of our self-definition as institutions of higher learning. What is a university, what is academic freedom, and how do people with different worldviews come together in the pursuit of knowledge? These are the questions I hope to address today as I consider the problem of campus regulation of racist, sexist, and homophobic speech.

First, I believe we should read the Constitution and the Bill of Rights as a whole. The values of equality and personhood run throughout our founding document. Equality of access and equality of participation are ideals that are central to and definitive of American democracy, particularly in the twentieth century. Hate speech on campus cuts deeply into equality of access for minority group members. To understand this, it is necessary to look at both the quantity and the quality of hate activity on campus. The quantity has increased to the point where few students of color can expect to go through four years of undergraduate education without encountering hate speech. By hate speech I refer to speech the only function of which is to wound and degrade by asserting the inherent inferiority of a group. Similarly, few women will leave our universities without encountering sexual harassment in the form of unwanted advances or a hostile environment created by sexist comments, pornography, or misogynist speech.

Exposure to these kinds of hate leaves lasting impressions on university students who come to the academy at a formative time in their lives. Students are a population particularly at risk for psychological harm. Younger students are forming their identities, abandoning old peer ties, and seeking out new ones. They are in a transitional stage vis-à-vis families, coming to new understanding about what is good and bad in relationships with parents and siblings; playing out old dramas of interpersonal relationships with new characters; seeking self-knowledge; and considering what they want to do with their adult lives. Older students face the financial uncertainty and self-doubt that comes from returning to school. Many students – younger and older – are economically at risk, holding down part-time jobs, taking out loans, and hoping for financial aid. Some have partners or children or parents whom they are supporting. Some are academically at risk, unsure about how to make it in the maze of large classes, inaccessible professors, fancy-talking classmates, and cultural or class differences that make up the academic world. Even those excelling academically face self-doubt generated by examinations, grades, and job interviewing. Many emotional disorders manifest for the first time in college. Coming to the university is a major life stress event.

This is not the time to subject someone to psychological assault. It is not the time for a student to come back to her dorm room and find an anonymous note calling her ancestors filth, not a time for a student to come to class and find posters advocating the genocide of everyone of his religion, not a time to walk down the street and face shouts and threats and demeaning and hateful things said about one's body. The administrators and counselors on the front lines of dealing with students, those who know about the students who have changed majors, moved out of the dorm, dropped classes, gone into therapy, and left the university because of harassment know that the problem is a serious one.

A student in Texas told me of studying in her carrel at the library, getting up for a break, and coming back to find someone had drawn swastikas in the margin of her textbook and on her notes.

Another woman, a white woman, told me of walking to school with her moot court partner, an African-American woman, when a passing motorist called out, "Get that n___ bitch off this campus."

A student writer at UCLA spoke of sitting in class listening to a lecture and discovering that someone had written on the wall next to her desk, "Kill all the jews."

On their way to a reception in my honor when I received tenure at UCLA, students who rode the elevator were confronted with graffiti that said, "I want Asian c_nt."

In each of these cases, students were participating in essential activities and daily life at the university—studying, walking to class, listening to the lecture, or attending a social event—when they were attacked out of the blue with a hateful and degrading message. They were ambushed, making the space that once seemed familiar and safe seem threatening and not one's own.

These students are supposed to keep functioning, and most of them do. Look away from the death threat, refocus on the lecture, and keep on taking notes. Turn the page, keep studying, ignore the swastikas. Continue down the street with your moot court partner, do not be late for class, and forget that someone felt compelled to threaten you and hate you in a public and aggressive way. Feel your knees go weak when the stranger yells from the car and keep walking, head erect, like you have a right to be there.

People manage, but they manage under a burden. Maybe they do not hear all the lecture. Maybe they do not get a full night's sleep, and maybe they do not do as well on the calculus exam. There is a cost, a burden, a price paid for the epidemic of assaultive speech on our campuses, and the cost is paid disproportionately by historically subordinated groups.

The principles of equality and liberty recognize the worth of every human being and the right of each to participate in the institutions of our nation. As Professor Charles Lawrence has pointed out, the case of *Brown v. Board of Education*[2] was, at its core, a case about the way in which racist messages violate the rights of equality and liberty. In *Brown,* the court recognized that no matter how equal the schools, separating children on the basis of race was never constitutionally permissible. Why was this? We separate children all the time, by district, by birth date, and by ability. The reason it was not permissible to separate children by race was that segregation represented a racist ideology. Jim Crow embodied white supremacy: white is pure and must remain untainted by the dirt, by the filth, of the Other. The Supreme Court knew this when it decided *Brown,* and it considered substantial testimony about the psychological harm caused by segregation. Separate is never equal, the court found, because of the damage caused by *the message* of racial inferiority. *Brown* thus sets up a set of competing values at odds with the protection of racist speech.

In addition to the liberty and equality interests implicated by hate-speech regulations, there are also First Amendment reasons to ban hate speech. The goal of the First Amendment is to protect dissent, to maximize public discourse, and to achieve the great flowering of debate and of ideas that we need for democracy to work. Hate speech impedes these goals because hate speech is intended to and has the effect of cutting off

debate. When someone calls you a hate name, they are not trying to get into a debate or even a rancorous argument with you.
They are telling you that you are less than human, that you have
no right to be here, and that your speech is worthless. The typical responses to racist hate speech include fear, flight, or
fistfights. People use these words precisely because of the
wounding, silencing effect. I suggest that there are some forms
of speech we need to limit precisely because we value speech.

Let me give you some examples of hate speech limiting free
speech. One of my students was discussing gay-rights issues with
friends in a restaurant. A stranger came up to him and said ag-
gressively, "Are you a f_gg_t?" My student said, yes, he is gay
and proud of it. Then the assailant escalated his verbal abuse,
finally assaulting my student physically. Since the incident, the
student tells me, his friends look over their shoulders and size up
the room before they discuss gay issues. They speak in hushed
tones; sometimes they do not speak. In this case, responding to
hate speech with counterspeech resulted in physical assault.

Because physical abuse so often follows verbal abuse in our
violent and patriarchal culture, it does not require actual physical assault for assaultive speech to silence. In San Francisco's
Chinatown, community members who testified at a public hearing, many of them participating in the political process for the
first time, found that their names and a racist, anti-Asian message were broadcast on the White Aryan Resistance hotline.[3]
Many of the speakers feared for their lives. They will think twice
before testifying again.

Any university professor who has tried to promote classroom
discussion about race, gender, and homosexuality knows how
hard it is to get students to express their ideas, feelings, and dis-

agreements about these topics. Our ability to speak across cultural divides is impeded by the feelings of animosity growing on our campuses. Hate speech shuts down conversations and keeps us from the important work of learning to talk across difference.

Let me emphasize that I believe in the First Amendment. It is absolutely critical, particularly in these days of economic collapse, that citizens retain the right of dissent, the right to criticize the government. In suggesting that the ugliest forms of hate speech should fall outside First Amendment protection, I make a distinction between dissent, or criticism directed against the powerful institutions that affect our lives, and hate speech, or speech directed against the least powerful segment of our communities.

It is the lawyer's job to make distinctions in principled ways, and the principle I suggest is that of antisubordination. Our minority students are already at risk for a variety of historical reasons. Many of them come from economically disadvantaged backgrounds. Many are of the first generation in their families to go to college. The antisubordination principle recognizes the historical reality that some members of our community are less powerful and have less access to education. The universities have come a long way in recognizing this, making commitments to affirmative action and to outreach programs to help less advantaged students. Protecting these students from psychological attack is part of that same ethical goal of equal opportunity and inclusion.

Universities bear special obligations for several reasons. First, universities are part of the public trust. They receive government support in the form of subsidies and tax advantages. State universities are supported by taxpayers—by all taxpayers, including the working poor and immigrants who are less often the beneficiaries of a university education. Second, university students are a captive audience. Students cannot choose not to come to class, not to go to their mailboxes, and not to study in the library. When hate speech invades the campus, students have no choice, no place to go to escape the speech. Students are encouraged to think of the university as their home. The university encourages activities in and out of class and promotes a host of extracurricular clubs and events that are critical to the educational experience. The physical confines of the campus are not the anonymous places that city streets are. They are home. And to have ugly messages of hate posted on the walls of a home is much more of an intrusion than, say, a racist march downtown. "Invasion" is a word often used by people who have received hate messages in their dorms, in their churches or synagogues, and in their homes. The right to a sense of personal security in the geographic confines of a home place is something we owe our students.

Finally, universities are not neutral, relativistic, amoral institutions. They stand for something. They stand for the pursuit of knowledge. They stand for ethical striving. They stand for equal opportunity. We wave these values in letterheads, mottos, and catalogs used to recruit students. In the postmodern age it has become unfashionable to talk about truth, ethics, and morality in an absolute sense. Feminists and other critical scholars have shown that too often "truth" and "ethics" are constructions of powerful people intent on keeping their power. This critique is important, but it does not take away the core of what it means to be a university. We are about the pursuit of knowledge and ethics. We do teach values.

We require of our faculty teaching, research, and service. We pay people to do this because we believe it helps realize certain goals we believe in. We forbid cheating in faculty research and publication, in student work, and in sports. We seek excellence, reward effort, and extol critical thinking. A teacher who comes to class unprepared, a student who plagiarizes on a term paper, or an administrator who absconds with funds – any number of people who do not meet our standards – will encounter sanctions.

It is odd to me that the idea that we stand for certain standards of behavior is commonplace and acceptable in these areas but completely contestable when it comes to hate speech, sexual harassment, or bigotry. Suddenly, when it is suggested that harassing women, students of color, gays and lesbians, or Jews is wrong, a great chorus of relativists arises.

"We cannot condemn this behavior because that is not our role," I have been told. "We are not cops. Leave this behavior to private sanction." Some have even argued that private sanction is inappropriate, that a faculty member or an administrator merely expressing outrage at racist speech, without engaging in disciplinary action, has a chilling effect on speech and is therefore inappropriate.

The media rage of PC bashing fuels this myth that people have a "right" to say assaultive things to each other. A law student at Stanford who said to a gay man, "Die, f_gg_t, I hope you die of AIDS," says that he is a victim of political correctness when students and faculty criticize his homophobia. A UCLA fraternity that published a songbook with lyrics calling for the mutilation of women's bodies with graters and chainsaws is defended on First Amendment ground. The First Amendment is used to valorize such behavior, to make it seem like heroic resistance to PC orthodoxy rather than what it is: a cowardly capitulation to the group thinking of patriarchy and homophobia. Anyone who engages in such verbal assault deserves and should expect condemnation in the strongest possible terms. There is a campaign on the right to call condemnation of such behavior "thought policing," "PC," or interfering with the freedom of harassers to do as they please.

When I speak out against hate speech and harassment, I intend to affect hate behavior. I intend to deter it and to protect the many students who are victimized by it. To condone hate speech is to encourage it. It teaches our students that doing nothing in the face of persecution is ethically sound.

A belief in human dignity is at the heart of what we do. Why else try to study and to know all the phenomena of the universe if we do not believe, ultimately, in the glory of life on this planet and the grace of knowing all we can about how to live decent lives while we are here? There is no value-free reason for our existence. We do stand for human dignity, and we must protect the dignity of each of our students.

What about the dignity of the perpetrator—the professor who is confused about his role, who asks a student out on a date not realizing the pain it will lead to? The frustrated monocultural student who lashes out when confronted with cultural difference? The fraternity member who gets drunk and does something hateful, urged on by peer pressure, that he is later ashamed of? I hope that in our response to hate speech we will respect fully the rights and the personhood of these individuals. Any regulations we enact must, of course, provide maximum due process and must take full account of mitigating circumstances.

Nonregulation abandons the humanity of the perpetrators by accepting their assaultive behavior as the best they can do. In setting standards of humane behavior and proclaiming that we believe everyone in our community can attain those standards, we bring the racist, the sexist, and the homophobe back into the community. They may not change, in one short lifetime, all the dark places of their learned bigotry, but they will learn an important, functional lesson about what society expects in school, in the workplace, and in the community. I would not deprive a student of a chance to learn this at the university, before he or she goes out into the unforgiving world.

For all our students, then, for both the attacked and the attacker, setting institutional standards is important. Perpetrators are victims of structures of subordination as well. I believe men are victims of patriarchy. I do not mean to say that their victimization is the same as that of women. Of course it is not. I just mean that the batterer, the date-raper, the pornography addict, the man who thinks he has to attack another man with a baseball bat in order to prove his manhood, the ones who drink themselves silly every weekend rather than confronting and expressing their feelings and fears – these men live lives diminished by the pervasive poison of patriarchy. To the extent that these men are our students and colleagues, I hope we can act proactively through consciousness raising, through community discussion of guidelines for behavior, through expanding the curriculum to increase knowledge about subordination, and through affirmative action to increase cross-cultural interaction so that we can reach perpetrators as well as victims.

The unfortunate pattern of response to hate speech has been to do nothing until a serious incident creates a crises. The crises is then followed by hastily enacted rules or, worse yet, ex post facto discipline. These hate incidents are not going to go away. The recent indications that the Republican party intends to exploit racial tensions in the next presidential election are just one hint among many that things are going to get worse, not better, and it will fall to us in the academy to try to pick up the pieces of social dislocation and hate that lands on our manicured academic lawns. I urge that we do the foundational work now. We need to start by gathering information. Every campus should have a system for collecting data about hate incidents. We should provide fora for students to speak out about the discrimination they feel. We need to share this information among campuses, to get a clear picture of the extent of the problem, and to develop proactive strategies for dealing with hate. I believe we should draft narrow regulations that will penalize the worst forms of assaultive speech, and I would challenge those who disagree with me to come up with concrete alternative responses to hate speech, including strong nondisciplinary condemnation of bigotry, affirmative action programs, curriculum reform, and other means to improve the campus climate for underrepresented groups. There is a range of alternatives open to us, and I hope we continue to debate and consider them all.

The theme of this lecture is academic freedom. I began by telling you that in urging restriction of hate speech and sexual harassment I was told such restrictions impinge on academic freedom. Academic freedom must include freedom from racist and sexist oppression unless we mean that academic freedom is the sole property of the powerful. I think that the origin of the concept is exactly the opposite. It was the freedom to say that the planets revolve around the sun, even when the church insisted it was the other way around. It was the freedom to expose government corruption, even when the government is paying your salary. This courageous tradition is one we must preserve. It is not the same as the freedom to hurt and degrade the powerless.

Many will disagree with what I have said. I hope we can continue to argue with and learn from one another, letting our speech fill the space made by academic freedom.

---

1   See, e.g., Nadine Strossen, "Regulating Racist Speech on Campus: A Modest Proposal?" *Duke Law Journal* (1990): 484.
2   347 U.S. 483 (1954); Charles R. Lawrence III, "If He Hollers Let Him Go: Regulating Racist Speech on Campus," in Mari Matsuda et al., *Words That Wound* (Boulder, Colo.: Westview Press, 1993).
3   Author's conversation with attorney Dennis Hayashi.

11

CHANGE, BACKLASH, AND LEARNING TO TALK

The universities are a battlefield in what some are calling the "culture wars." This is no surprise. Contrary to the dismissive metaphor of the ivory tower, universities are centers of thought and action. When a dictator plans a coup to end democratic governance, he includes in his plan a way to shut down, or at least shut up, the university. The contest over knowledge has life-and-death consequences. In the late 1980s, an attack on multiculturalism, social history, women's studies, and other academic innovations achieved national attention.[1] Members of the Law and Society Association, an organization dedicated to the interdisciplinary study of law as a living, human creation, were sometimes targets of this attack. This talk at the association's annual meeting was part of a 1990 plenary on the postcolonial university, intended to analyze and respond to the culture wars.

PATTERNS OF CHANGE AND BACKLASH

Law-and-society scholars already know about change and backlash. You know what happens sometimes to scholars who challenge disciplinary boundaries; who call attention to hidden ideology; who say law is connected to history, politics, and economy; and who see history, politics, and economy in low-level, social manifestations as well as in the activities of elites. This kind of work is threatening, and it generates a range of disciplinary actions that some of you are all too familiar with.

There is an analogy between institutional and interpersonal backlash. What we learn from looking at families and interpersonal relationships is that change is risk. In a dysfunctional relationship, parties on all sides are often invested in maintaining the dysfunction. When one member tries to break out of old patterns, others will engage in "change-back" tactics to maintain the status quo. A child asserts herself against overbearing parents and finds herself suddenly accused of not loving them. An addict takes the first step to recovery, and his caretaking partner is suddenly withdrawn and depressed. A battered woman threatens to leave the batterer and finds that the violence escalates. She may even lose her life.

What we learn from studying change and backlash in the context of subordination is that changes in conditions of domination are usually generated from the oppressed rather than the oppressor. Both sides in a relationship of subordination have some investment in the status quo, but the superordinate beneficiary more predictably plays the change-back game, a game in which the subordinate is tempted to concede.

Consider the example of the academy. In the 1960s, outsiders demanded access to education. In the 1970s, they demanded access to *relevant* education, and after a series of student strikes at places like Harvard and San Francisco State, new disciplines joined the academy: Afro-American studies, Asian-American studies, and Chicano studies. The sister discipline, Women's Studies, followed closely. The demand for inclusion was first,

"Let us sit in your classrooms," and second, "Give us a separate space to develop our identity, our history, our theory."

In the 1980s we stepped further toward the postcolonial university. It was not enough for feminism to exist only in women's studies or for race/culture analysis to remain cabined in ethnic studies. In every discipline – history, science, literature, and law – the upstart newcomers asked, "How would the entire universe of truth as presently constructed change if the worldviews of various nonelite groups were taken seriously?" That question posed a serious challenge to academic legitimacy that generated backlash from the previously privileged. As Catharine MacKinnon put it, "The anxiety about engaged theory is particularly marked among those whose particularities formed the prior universal."[2]

The anxiety is expressed in numerous ways. We have the bumper crop of academic nostalgia books, lamenting the loss of real scholarship, real literacy, and real (western) culture. We have the "reasoned arguments" that reflect anxiety about the claims of subordinated groups: anti-affirmative action rhetoric and the revival of biological determinism and social Darwinism, often delivered in a "shoot to kill" style of argumentation that barely masks a seething rage.

Even more overt backlash is on the rise in the academy: students and faculty of color, gays and lesbians, women, Jews, and others are increasingly subject to terrorism on campus in the form of hate speech and violence. Organized harassment campaigns, including planted provocateurs in classes; disinformation; externally funded right-wing student newspapers that target minority scholars; and a growing network of pseudo-scholarly organizations running ads, holding conferences, and sending out newsletters attacking the integrity of feminists and scholars of colors. If you have not seen this yet, it is coming soon to a campus near you.

People of color are regularly subject to ambushes, or unexpected psychological aggression that has the effect of reminding them that they are "tenants at sufferance." African-American students at the University of Michigan, for example, told me they are regularly stopped by the Ann Arbor police. A student at Stanford from an immigrant background was told by a classmate, "It's not fair that because you're here, some white man had to go to Davis." On a hunch, I asked her, "What was your undergraduate GPA?" "4.0 at Berkeley," she said.

When racist comments are made, they are made within a culture that gives these words special power. The students at Dartmouth who called an African-American professor a "welfare queen" drew on a cultural capital well known to themselves and their target. Their message was, "Our degrading image of you is coextensive with your definition in this society, and we will use that image to annihilate you." Increasingly, scholars of color are asked to get up every morning to teach, knowing that such messages are fresh in students' minds. Women are expected to return each semester to teach after reading student evaluations that attack their clothing and speculate on their sex lives.

In addition to psychological ambush, material barriers to change are also on the rise. Tuition is up, loans and grants are down, and academic support for oppositional scholarship is disappearing. Funding is increasingly governed by commitment to a conservative agenda, from private foundations that require laissez-faire economic allegiance to government funds reserved for defense research. An interesting form of material backlash is the recent phenomenon of conferring star status, honoraria, book contracts, and grants to people of color who are willing to attack their own.[3] Add to this the statistics showing that faculty from subordinated groups are more often lecturers, untenured, disproportionately underpaid, more often working at institutions with high teaching demands, and subject to increasingly stringent standards for tenure, promotion, and outside review, all of which just happen to coincide with the recent limited entrée created by affirmative action, and a picture emerges of students and faculty from formerly excluded groups trying to teach and learn under increasingly difficult material circumstances.

In outlining these mechanisms, I mean to suggest that the escalation of the backlash in the 1980s was not an accident. The moment when the conservatives took control of the federal government coincided with the moment when the most powerful second-generation critiques of heterosexist, white, male, class-bound subjectivity came into theoretical flowering in every branch of the academy. This created a contradiction, a tension, that has propelled us into the 1990s on a wave of rising hatred and anxiety coupled with an emerging, genuinely multicultural, nationwide student protest movement. It is going to be our privilege in the 1990s to inhabit the academy in a time of change, risk, backlash, and, if we are lucky, a dramatic shift in the structure of knowledge that will make all our work more creative, engaged, and insightful than anything we have yet done.

RESPONSE TO BACKLASH

In response to backlash, victims often decide to leave the academy or to conform to its demands. I have sat in on discussions with feminists focusing on whether writing a doctrinal article or teaching from a more conventional syllabus might be the key to academic survival. A senior law-and-society scholar advised me in my first year of teaching, "Don't write a legal history piece until you have tenure."

I benefited from the concern expressed in that advice – somebody wanted me to make it! – but I did not benefit from the substance. I knew that I could not be a pretend positivist or a temporary torts maven and that, if I tried to, I would never write a thing.

What I have learned from my own experience and from the message of the gay and lesbian community is that "silence equals death." It can affirmatively harm you to act as though conforming to the expectations of the academy as patriarch will save you from its wrath.

My way of dealing with backlash is to situate the backlash as historically inevitable, to talk about its patterns, and to work with organizations and networks that are prepared to take on power. I work for formal institutional responses, including rules against sexual harassment and hate speech. I try to push myself and my students to think about private forms of intervention in structures of subordination that each of us, in our own daily lives, might choose to engage in.

CONSCIOUSNESS RAISING, LEARNING TO TALK, AND INTERVENTION

The method I find most useful for thinking about intervention is consciousness raising, or CR. Now, those of you from the serious East may have some preconceived notion of CR as an overly indulgent West Coast group therapy that involves dramatic and weepy acts of self-revelation. The CR that Professor

Rosaldo[4] and I used with students was much more modest than that. We asked questions like, "Describe something you remember from childhood about how you learned gender roles"; "Describe a time you heard a racist, sexist, anti-Semitic, or homophobic comment"; "What, if anything, did you do?" "What happened?" Students generated their own questions. An African-American woman said one day, "I'd like to ask my white classmates, When was the last time you were told you are articulate?" No white student recalled being called articulate, but several students of color did. They talked about being told they write and speak well and about how this made them feel that they were being implicitly divided from "the rest of your people who are not as smart as you."

Opening up a space to talk nonconfrontationally about race, gender, and sexuality turned the students into teachers. Students told funny but troubling stories of mistaken identity. A black or Chicano man in a tux is asked for an ashtray or a glass of water at a formal event. A woman in a law firm is subject to the assumption that she is there to type and take messages.

The format we used for CR was sitting in a circle, each person speaking in turn around the circle with no interruptions allowed. Because of the variety of linguistic styles, we felt this formal procedure was important. Some of the best input came from students who needed time to think before they spoke and who would not have entered the fray in a crossfire discussion. Our CR sessions were all voluntary and outside class time, and many students reported that it was the best part of the class.

I came to think of our CR sessions as "learning to talk." Our students, like ourselves, often come to the academy culturally deprived. They grow up in segregated settings, and they rarely talk across racial lines. Men and women do not talk openly and open-mindedly about sex, sexuality, and gender. Straights and gays do not talk together about sexual choices. We are all deprived of knowledge and insights that can come only from learning to talk to each other. I thought I knew a lot about racist and sexist speech, but white men, I have found, have heard things I have never heard. They know things about the objectification of women in ordinary day-to-day conversations in male-only settings that I can only learn if: (1) I talk to them and (2) they talk to me with consciousness of their race/sex position and an awareness of the feminist perspective.

Here is a CR question for this gathering: "Recall a time when you heard a discussion about a colleague who is a white woman, a woman of color, or a man of color implicitly or explicitly questioning their ability. How did you respond?" I ask this question because of a pattern of undermining that affects people I care about. An African-American state senator from Selma, Alabama, is under investigation for alleged criminal acts and ethical violations. In seeking help, he finds that mainstream civil rights organizations hesitate. They want the "real facts" before they decide whether to support him. Once he stands accused by the local bar, he is no longer presumed innocent. This is hardly surprising in a country where the function of the criminal justice system has been largely to create in the public mind an equation between "Black" and "criminal."

In the past few weeks on the Stanford campus, a series of redbaiting allegations have plagued a distinguished Asian-American scholar hired after a long and aggressive search. Before this man even arrived to teach, exposés appeared in the student paper alleging that the scholar belongs to a revolutionary political group that has infiltrated various student organizations. Accusations that certain students and staff also belong to that group generated growing confusion. The presumption was not that this scholar's well-deserved reputation should rest conclusively on his work or that student activists' expressions of outrage at the lack of diversity in the faculty represent their real agenda. Instead, the allegations were taken seriously. That the image of sneaky, mysterious, underground, third-world organizations is given credence is hardly surprising in a society in which the dominant media stereotype of Asians is inscrutability.

Another portrait of undermining is one that Richard Delgado suggests with the slightly paranoid accuracy that marks much of his work. Imagine, he asks, a student, white and male, dropping by to see a professor, also white and male, for a beginning-of-the-year chat. "So what are you taking?" the professor asks. "Fed. courts, tax, evidence, and feminist legal theory with Ms. Visitor." (Ms. Visitor is a woman of color, and, in fact, that is not an inaccurate generic name for women of color in many law schools.) "Tell me about feminist legal theory," the professor asks. "Well," the student says, "so far the discussions have been pretty unfocused."

What is going on here? In that moment the student is testing the water. It is only the first week of school. He has not formed a fixed opinion of Ms. Visitor or of the class. The professor, whether conscious of it or not, has created a moment deeply infused with the politics of power. When he hears the student test the water, he can say one of several things. He can say, "We hired Ms. Visitor because she is known as a brilliant theoretician and an excellent teacher. If the discussions seem unfocused, I'd take careful note of the questions she asks. I bet you'll start to see the connections emerge." Or he can say, "Oh, really?" and with a look of concerned curiosity, "Tell me more." Or he can say, with an air of passing on insider secrets, "Well, I can't understand this obsession with sexuality that seems to permeate her work. All she seems to think about is sex."

Professor Delgado suspects that hundreds of conversations like this go on in the beginning of every term. Students uncertain about new kinds of teachers put out feelers, look for permission to attack, and press many buttons to find which path offers the least resistance to their expressions of anxiety and rage.

Senior faculty can take the role of opinion leaders in supporting white feminists, women of color, men of color, and radical reform in curricula and pedagogy. Even the neutrality of "Oh, really? Tell me more" passes on the message that the jury is still out, that there is no presumption that the visitor has a right to stay past teatime.

In preparing this panel, we came up with the metaphor of the green card. As scholars of color, we feel as though our presence in the academy is akin to the legalized noncitizen. "You can live here, but don't get too comfortable." Becoming a citizen means passing a test in cultural norms, denying one's own indigenous knowledge, abandoning one's home locations, and naturalizing the dominant worldview in one's own body and soul and teaching and scholarship.

A postcolonial university is one in which the formerly colonized can teach and learn, study and write, without abandoning their culture. It is one in which the objects of so much of our study – the poor, Native people, working people, women of all races, and men of color – will make up more than just the topics of research. They will make up not only the students who are allowed to listen to the lectures but also the full citizenry, studying, writing, and producing knowledge in an academic world that has recognized their claim to citizenship.

Commitment to this vision of the university is my work, and it is a privilege to share this work with you. It is inevitable, I think, that organizations like the Law and Society Association will take a leading role as we tumble toward the much-touted multicultural century.

With its eye on interdisciplinary study and its distrust of frozen formalisms, the law-and-society movement was founded with a renegade vision. Intellectual excitement over a changing world, and changing understandings of that world, makes the scholars in this room less needy of the turf-protecting change-back game.

The intellectual strength of the law-and-society movement is its rejection of narrow conceptualization. At the core, both law and society and multiculturalism understand that culture exists and that law operates within culture. Both are about exploding formalism and expanding knowledge thereby. That expanded space has made room for scholars like the three of us on this panel.[5] You have heard from us. We would like to hear from you.[6] In our conversations, let us abandon the easy consensus of the days when we feigned homogeneity, taking instead the difficult and risky road of honest talk transcending, without obliterating, difference.

---

1   For an excellent discussion of this assault, see Lawrence Levine, *The Opening of the American Mind* (Boston: Beacon Press, 1996).

2   Catharine MacKinnon, *Toward a Feminist Theory of the State* (Cambridge: Harvard University Press, 1989), p. xv.

3   See, e.g., Dinesh D'Souza, *The End of Racism: Principles for a Free Society* (New York: Free Press, 1995); and Shelby Steele, *The Content of Our Character: A New Vision of Race in America* (New York: HarperPerennial, 1991).

4   Professor Renato Rosaldo, an anthropologist at Stanford University, was a copanelist at this plenary and my coteacher at Stanford Law School in a class called "Subordination, Traditions of Thought, and Experience."

5   The third panelist was Professor Charles R. Lawrence III.

6   The meeting then divided into small groups for CR sessions.

12

*Because I have argued for restrictions on racist, homophobic, and misog-
ynist speech, people assume I am not a civil libertarian. In fact, I am
deeply committed to the civil liberties tradition and support the work of
organizations like the ACLU. I oppose a version of civil liberties that
fails to recognize how poverty, patriarchy, racism, homophobia, and class
oppression deny the very rights that the Bill of Rights enshrines. This
speech,[1] at a conference organized by feminists at Temple University and
the University of Pennsylvania, attempts to identify that part of the civil
libertarian tradition that goes beyond formalistic and apolitical conceptions
of rights.*

Somewhere tonight, in this city, a woman will pay with her
body the price of patriarchy. With a fist to her face, with her
sweat and terror, once again she will learn the lesson of her value
in this world, as she did as a child, when she first asked the meaning of the word "rape," as she turned that meaning over in her
head, thinking, how can this be? What world do I live in that
this could happen to me because I am female? Rape, as we say
theoretically, is constructed. It is not necessary. It is created by
an idea we call patriarchy. It is created by an idea that combines

sex and violence and domination. It is created by ideas expressed in pornography. Ideas, in the cosmology of traditional civil liberties, are sacred. The question I address tonight is this: What are progressive civil liberties? As women who care about women, as human beings who care about human beings, what do we need to keep in the civil liberties tradition, and what do we need to challenge?

When I open by reminding myself that women pay a real concrete and bloody price for patriarchy, I mean that as a deliberate starting point for critiquing the civil liberties tradition. In that tradition, the price metaphor is central. We speak of "paying the price" for freedom. By starting with women, with all the women in this room and our knowledge that we are walking targets in a misogynist world, I want to call attention to an equally important price: the price of systems of oppression. As ethical human beings, we strive to end oppression. We strive to end the poverty that left homeless mothers with infants trudging through the melting snow in Washington, D.C., where I live, this past winter. We strive to end the quiet violence of racism, of homophobia, of sexism, and of workplace exploitation that steals the joy of life from beautiful bodies.

We are warned, as we seek to end these ills, of another price: the cost to civil liberties that may come with aggressive eradication of social ills. This warning is raised by both good-faith and bad-faith critics. In suggesting legal limits to assaultive speech – limits to hate propaganda that is directed against traditionally disempowered groups and that has the effect of excluding them from the workplace, from getting an education, and from other opportunities and liberties – I have met and argued with many critics. There are good-faith critics, like a feminist socialist I spoke with a few weeks ago, who said, "I've thought about what you're saying and I just can't agree with you because I don't trust the state and I don't want to give the state the power to censor. However harmful some speech may be to me, I fear the greater harm of state coercion."

I have also met bad-faith critics. I have come to recognize these critics by their rage. However tentative and complexified I try to make my arguments for limiting assaultive speech, I have come across the angry civil libertarian who acts as though I have stepped on his toes. This person yells. He uses language like "fascist," "thought police," "how dare you," "politically correct," and "you people don't realize that you're the ones who need the First Amendment the most." Another favorite rhetorical tool in this person's arsenal is the "poor other guy over there," a professor at some school who is no longer teaching because he was taunted by students who called him racist or another professor whose reputation was ruined by charges of sexual harassment. At some point in the conversation, I realize that I am actually talking to the "other guy": to someone enraged and confused by the changes taking place around him, angry at the invaders who challenge his speech with their own. This feels to him like the end of freedom.

At bottom, these critics, both the good and the bad faith, set up an inevitable coupling of aggressive eradication of oppression with a loss of civil liberties. If we have rules against assaultive speech, against pornography, against sexual harassment, we are on the road to a police state. If we promote new social conventions that stigmatize bigotry, we introduce mind control. This coupling comes up in other areas troubling to feminists. If we restrict abortion clinic protest, do we endanger dissent? If we demand diligent prosecution of rape, do we inflate the power of a corrupt criminal justice system? It is not my intent to dismiss these concerns – they are real. I intend to ask what we, as feminists, as progressives, might make of the civil liberties tradition.

Traditional civil liberties feel traditionally male to me. The tradition is tough, smart, and defiant. The state is the bad father – the tough guy – and the traditional civil libertarian is even tougher than the state. He is willing to feel the burn, to pay the price of freedom. There is an elitism here – this tradition is intentionally counterintuitive and not for the masses. The poor average chumps who cannot take it or do not get it will never understand why the criminal must go free, why the swastika has to fly, or why the child pornographer must keep his millions to maintain liberty for all.

When I swore allegiance to this tradition as a young person, I felt special because I got it. I could stand up and argue for the exclusionary rule while classmates and neighbors shouted outrage that a guilty person could go free. My hero was a mythical, leather-jacketed ACLU lawyer, on motorcycle, defending drug dealing, protest, and pornography, smashing the state wherever it dared to wrest power from the people. Later I learned – and, mind you, this is a prototype, so do not think I am talking about anyone you might know – that Mr. Leather Jacket was exploiting his secretary and his girlfriend, that the drug money supported right-wing death squads, and that the pornographer was filming rape and calling it free love. Just as there is no easy walk to freedom, there are no easy civil liberties.

The critical thinking that civil libertarians champion forces us to question the conventions of dominant civil libertarian thought. A key device in this school of thought is the neutral, absolute rule. We do not ban speech regardless of whom it harms, because we are safe only with absolute rules that protect all speech. Discernment is impossible and dangerous. Absolutism protects us from the creeping tyranny that exceptions create. All speech must be free for the speech we value to remain free. Therefore, the pornographer and the antiwar protester, the clinic defender and those who would close down the clinic, are treated the same.

How does this traditional view meet the test of history? Not very well, I think. If we look at American history, we find that, first of all, absolute protection of speech has never been available to the citizens of this land. Every time — every single time — people have challenged existing power with any degree of success, they have been prosecuted, persecuted, sabotaged, and silenced by the state. Protection of effective dissent is not a hallmark of our legal system. You can pick up any labor history text and know this. This history creates a longing for absolutism. If only we could forbid the state from ever touching our speech. Unfortunately, rules against speech code could not have prevented what the police did to the Panthers. The absolutist view asks us to give up the ability to attack dangerous verbal assaults in exchange for something we could never have, at least not under present conditions: noninterference with progressive speech.

Another hallmark of the traditional civil liberties analysis is the public/private distinction. It is the state, the bad father, that the traditional civil libertarian fears. The threat to liberty comes from the state. Private systems of violence and oppression are not, therefore, a primary concern. Under present law and according to most traditional civil libertarians, the state may not punish you for what you say, but a private employer may. This distinction hurts the cause of progressive speech. State and private suppression of liberty have always worked in tandem such that a program of civil liberties that ignores private suppression of speech will never achieve its ends. Workers are silenced in the workplace because they need jobs. Women are silenced at home by violence, by abuse, by incest, and by the message that their ideas have little value and that if they speak no one will listen. Citizens are silenced by a corporate communications monopoly that limits access to effective speech.

All these silencings are private. When the state acts to suppress speech, it often uses private actors as a cover. You may be familiar with the history of Klan and police cooperation in the post-Reconstruction South, with the many private employers who were induced by the FBI to fire employees during the McCarthy period, and with the mercenary Pinkertons who shot striking workers while the police conveniently looked the other way. I see the neo-Nazis and cross burners of our day as direct inheritors of this tradition. Their goal is to harass, silence, threaten, and exclude. When the Aryan Nation thugs put your name on their computerized hit list after you write a letter to the editor supporting affirmative action, their intent is to end your speech. We get less speech, not more, when this kind of private silencing is seen as beyond the reach of the law.

In my view, progressive civil libertarians recognize private as well as public coercion as a threat to freedom. They operate not in terms of neutral absolute rules but in the context of the history and the culture that are ours. We are capable of discernment, of telling a cross burner from an anitwar protester, a corporate monopolist from a striking worker.

Unlike current law, progressive civil liberties will see the elimination of systems of oppression as a primary goal, as a prerequisite to freedom. This kind of civil liberties will include, therefore, a range of economic rights in its platform. In addition, it will apply all rules with reference to how those rules affect immediate relations of domination and subordination. I do not claim credit for inventing this version of civil liberties. Within the civil liberties and civil rights communities, there have always been factions arguing for this expanded view. Within fine organizations like the ACLU, the debate continues over the role of substantive economic rights in the civil liberties cause.

What the traditional and the progressive views share is a respect for the individual, a tolerance of difference, a belief that democracy requires engaged critical inquiry. In the abstract, these are important values. In the specific, we cannot avoid giving life to these values through a deep analysis of the world that we live in. Absolutism is not enough.

Let me try some examples. When a scared teenager trying to get an abortion must run a gauntlet of bloody photos, human tissue in jars, and screams of "baby killer," absolutism is not enough. The simple civil liberties answer is that words, images, pickets, epithets, and screams are speech; if it is speech, it is protected – the woman loses. Feminists insist that we add the social context: Who has the power here? Certainly not this young woman who comes to the clinic out of desperation. We live in a world in which women are still struggling for control over their own bodies, for choice in their reproductive lives, and for a share of political power. We live in a world in which the state has refused to offer women any assistance in the birthing and rearing of children: no paid maternity leave, no child care, and in many cases no job and no housing. This is not an easy case. The man blocking the clinic entrance screaming "baby killer" might look a lot like the man outside the factory entrance screaming "scab." If we press the mute button and remove all identifying characteristics, we will not be able to tell them apart. But this is not how to make hard choices in a cruel world. We cannot pretend not to know who is screaming what, to whom, in what context, and with what result. Absolutist free speech analysis would give us an easy answer, a fast answer, but it would require that we ignore the reality facing women who are turned away from clinics. When feminists hold up coat hangers and say "never again," they are reminding us that women's bodies are on the line in this debate. Free-speech neutrality must confront that coat hanger.

Here is another example. The Supreme Court has held that businesses have a privacy right, including the right to exclude safety inspectors who arrive unannounced at a job site to see whether safety regulations are being violated.[2] The Court held that inspectors have to obtain a warrant in advance.[3] The predictable result is that safety rules are often ignored until that rare event, that is, the arrival of the inspector with warrant in hand. I have talked to workers who are told to put their safety shoes on only when the inspector is coming. There is good reason to promote rules against random searches and to require warrants. Some would argue that we have to follow this rule for factory owners as well as for home owners and ordinary citizens to keep the arbitrariness of the state at bay. The progressive civil liberties I seek would again ask about history and social context: Who needs privacy and why? Whose body is on the line in the factory search case? Who holds the power? Anyone who has ever worked for a living in a factory or field or a fancy law firm knows how hard it is to complain about work conditions when you need your job. The power here is in the hands of the employer, magnified tenfold by the ten people who are standing in line for any halfway decent job in our present economy. We pay for the failure to enforce job safety rules in human limbs, in human lives. This, weighed against the privacy rights of fictitious legal entities, is real weight. There is more at stake, the traditionalists will argue. We must maintain the principle – the principle of privacy – and the absolute purity of that principle. No warrantless searches. If they search the factory today, then they will search the women's bookstore tomorrow and our bedrooms the day after. This is what I would like to ask the traditional civil libertarian: Is it inevitably impossible to draw a line, to consider the lives of working people, and to know that there is a difference between the factory and the bedroom?

A similar argument is made against the regulation of pornography and assaultive speech. "Who will decide?" I am asked by hostile and friendly critics alike. Who will decide which speech is assaultive, which speech harms, excludes, or degrades? My answers are several. I point out that the legal system is already deciding and has picked a long list of speech that is unprotected: false advertising, libel, slander, plagiarism, copyright infringement, fraud, and price-fixing conversations – I could go on and on. Present law restricts many kinds of speech, most often the kind of speech that interferes with business productivity or that harms the reputations and livelihoods of powerful people. We have already given up the power to decide.

Defining assaultive speech is a serious challenge, but difficulty of definition is not, standing alone, a reason to avoid the work. There are many definitional problems in law: defining a conversation in restraint of trade or identifying a text written with actual malice, for example, for purposes of defamation law. The fear of casting too wide a net in an effort to restrain harmful activity is a reason to maximize procedural and definitional safeguards. We do this all the time in law in areas that present subtle and seemingly intractable definitional challenges. We do this because we believe in the rule of law, in the ability to come up with reasoned distinctions that will target harmful activity without unduly limiting freedom. This is what we do in our legal system, however imperfectly. If definition of harmful speech is impossible, we are doing the impossible as we define slander, fraud, and other forms of restricted speech. If definition is impossible, period, then we might as well throw out the whole legal system and go back to the state of nature.

Despite my distrust of the "we can't define it" argument, I am sympathetic with the goal of absolutist protection. I respect the purist argument, exemplified in the dissents of Justice Hugo Black, that we should never restrict speech, including libelous speech. His goal was to preserve the dissent that is the living center of democracy. Unfortunately, even if Justice Black's absolutism had held the day, this would not have preserved dissent. By dissent I mean the protest of the powerless that is aimed at changing existing conditions of domination. There are absolute rules against shooting unarmed students engaged in peaceful protests. There are absolute rules against murdering political activists in their sleep. This has not made us safe. It is too easy for the police to say, as they do every day in urban America, "I thought he was reaching for a gun."

What will make us safe, then? As people who care about promoting dissent, what do we need? We need to address the prerequisites of dissent. If we care about ending political repression, we have to ask where repression comes from. This is where my work, I believe, intersects with Professor Lani Guinier's. She is writing about a deep understanding of democracy, not a democracy made up of simple mathematical rules, like winner take all, but a democracy rich with democracy's full promise to include each and every citizen in the governing of their own lives.[4] We need community control of police and prosecutors. We need widespread access to print and electronic media. We need literacy and a citizenry trained in critical thought. By critical thought, I do not mean, as is presently suggested, that we should have national standards that say if you know that three-fourths of the earth's surface is covered with water then you are a certified smart person. I mean we need to teach our children to ask questions and to seek answers with open and active minds. A populace capable of restraining the abuse of state power is what will preserve liberty. An educated, economically empowered populace – one guaranteed not only the right of dissent but also the right of access to effective speech, a populace subsidized and encouraged to exercise all human rights – is what will make speech free.

Here I want to address two particular problems that impede conversations like the one I am trying to start about the traditional notion of civil liberties. The first is confusion about what it means to think critically and with an open mind. The second is the problem for progressive people of our relationship to the state.

As to the first, when I say that I value dissent, critical inquiry, tolerance of diverse viewpoints, that is when the traditional civil libertarian will say, "Gotcha! Now you have to let the anti-Semites into the classroom, now you have to let the crosses burn, now you have to allow pornography in the workplace.

You said you wanted tolerance, open-mindedness, welcoming all views."

This is a challenge I would like to address. How can I say I am for critical thought when I am also for restricting assaultive speech? Is not all speech essential to critical inquiry? I think we have to be exactly that: critical. Letting a hundred voices speak at once is not necessarily the way to achieve critical thought. The goal of democratic free speech is to put conventional wisdom to the test, which requires rigor and sophistication. It requires discerning among genuine and spurious challenges. We do not have to include holocaust deniers in our history curriculum, because they are not about extending historical inquiry—they are about anti-Semitism. We do not have to let crosses burn, because they are not about debating race relation—they are about punishing, silencing, and running families out of their homes.

I have seen too many students confused by the claim that unless we let hate mongers into the room, critical inquiry will not take place. In fact, as a teacher, I have found that exactly the opposite is true. One of the hardest things to do in the classroom is to have honest, mutually critical discussions about racism, anti-Semitism, homophobia, and misogyny. We do not have enough of these discussions. We do not have models of how to have them, and a screaming match is the worst possible model. Hard-and-fast rules against name-calling and requiring listening before attacking are ways I have managed to get these discussions started in my classroom. I have also had to ask more than one student to remain in the room when they wanted to run out in tears. These are hard conversations, and pornography, anti-Semitic, racist, and homophobic epithets do not further critical, probing dialogue.

It is the value of speech I hope to promote by suggesting that we may need to limit some speech. This is indeed a paradox – no easy walk to freedom, no easy civil liberties.

The second paradox is our relationship to the state. We know enough about dirty tricks, disinformation, police crimes, and abuse of power to make us believe that the state is a bad idea, period. My father, a World War II veteran and a lifelong progressive, tells me that smashing the state is an infantile fantasy—it is pre-fascist. The belief that government can do no good was the Reagan-Bush excuse for doing no good, even when we knew we could. In my view, President Clinton's New Democrats threaten to continue this tradition. There are problems the state can solve easily. We are the richest country in the world, and we can provide decent housing, medical care, and education for all our citizens. We can make sure that no child goes hungry. It is dangerous to believe, as many of my good-hearted, compassionate students believe, that these are intractable problems, that the government would just mess things up further if it ever tried to do anything. We have not tried, and we have defunded the programs that we know work.

The citizenry needed to demand these things and has been silenced, disinformed, and excluded from power sharing. As a progressive civil libertarian, my job is twofold: to challenge abuses of state power and to demand state intervention to equalize power. To dream of absolute restraints on the state – no searches, no speech codes, and no fines for antichoice clinic protesters before we have worked to equalize power will mean only that power stays as presently distributed. I do not mean to denigrate absolutism as an ideal but only to challenge its simplistic, knee-jerk application.

It is a worthy ideal that we restrain the state. I am absolutist on certain things – torture, for one, killing, for another. I would support an absolute ban on the death penalty. Absolutism is a luxury, the luxury of not asking to whom, to what end, in what historical context, and with what present politics. It is so great to say, "I am against the death penalty, always, period, end of analysis. There is no case you could raise that would convince me to give the state the power to take the life of one of its citizens."

Unfortunately, there are too few times when this kind of easy, absolutist response is something I can sleep with. We are too far away from a perfect world, from a state we can trust, from a state that will wither away because it is us. Until then, we need to both urge the state to use its power to just ends and act to restrain the state when its power endangers us.

Somewhere tonight, in this city, a woman will pay the price of patriarchy. There is nothing natural, necessary, or inevitable about this. Freedom may cost, but the cost paid out in women's bodies is one we pay too unevenly to call it liberty. Let women share power. Let workers govern the workplace. Then let us decide whose body fairly bears the wounds that liberty may demand. Until then, too often, conventional civil liberties can mean only business as usual. Until then, too often, the powerful will impoverish their own lives and the lives of others, calling it liberty when they grab for themselves all earthly gain, calling it freedom when they walk over other human beings. As a feminist, I demand more from the civil liberties tradition than this. I remember the legions of workers, civil rights activists, union organizers, and antiwar protesters who have used the words "free speech" and "liberty" as words to an end, words with concrete promise, not neutral, detached abstractions that will protect us simply by their perfect purity but words we give meaning to in our daily struggles for decent lives.

1   Keynote Address at the Annenberg Center, Philadelphia, Pennsylvania, March 25, 1993.

2   *Marshall v. Barlow's Inc.*, 436 U.S. 307 (1978).

3   Ibid., 32

4   Lani Guinier, *The Tyranny of the Majority: Fundamental Fairness in Representative Democracy* (New York: The Free Press, 1994).

PART **III**

WE WILL NOT BE USED: *Asian American Identity*

13

The Asian Law Caucus is the original public interest law firm serving the Asian-American community. It was built up from scratch by young, radical lawyers who carried files in their car trunks and stayed up all night to type their own briefs. The Asian Law Caucus has changed the lives of many — poor and working people, immigrants, and troubled youth — the least advantaged in the Asian-American community. The Caucus has also made history, successfully bringing landmark cases that have changed the law and the legal system. The supporters of the Caucus include many who participated in the civil rights and antiwar movements and who have worked all their lives in coalition with other people of color. This history is what inspired the words below, delivered at a fund-raising banquet in April 1990.

It is a special honor to address supporters of the Asian Law Caucus. Here, before this audience, I am willing to speak in the tradition of our women warriors, to go beyond the platitudes of fund-raiser formalism and to talk of something that has been bothering me and that I need your help on. I want to speak of my fear that Asian Americans are in danger of becoming the racial bourgeoisie and of my resolve to resist that path.

Marx wrote of the economic bourgeoisie – of the small merchants, the middle class, and the baby capitalists who were deeply confused about their self-interest. The bourgeoisie, he said, often emulate the manners and ideology of the big-time capitalists. They are the "wannabes" of capitalism. Struggling for riches, often failing, confused about the reasons why, the economic wannabes go to their graves thinking that the big hit is right around the corner.

Living in nineteenth-century Europe, Marx thought mostly in terms of class. Living in twentieth-century America, in the land where racism found a home, I am thinking about race. Is there a racial equivalent of the economic bourgeoisie? I fear there may be, and I fear it may be us.

If white, as it has been historically, is the top of the racial hierarchy in America, and black, historically, is the bottom, will yellow assume the place of the racial middle? The role of the racial middle is a critical one. It can reinforce white supremacy if the middle deludes itself into thinking it can be just like white if it tries hard enough. Conversely, the middle can dismantle white supremacy if it refuses to be the middle, if it refuses to buy into racial hierarchy, and if it refuses to abandon communities of black and brown people, choosing instead to forge alliances with them.

The theme of the unconventional fund-raiser talk you are listening to is "we will not be used." It is a plea to Asian Americans to think about the ways in which our communities are particularly susceptible to playing the worst version of the racial bourgeoisie role.

I remember my mother's stories of growing up on a sugar plantation on Kauai. She tells of the Portuguese *luna,* or overseer. The *luna* rode on a big horse and issued orders to the Japanese and Filipino workers. The *luna* in my mother's stories is a tragic/comic figure. He thinks he is better than the other workers, and he does not realize that the plantation owner considers the *luna* subhuman, just like all the other workers. The invidious stereotype of the dumb "portagee" persists in Hawaii today, a holdover from the days of the *luna* parading around on the big horse, cloaked in self-delusion and false pride.

The double tragedy for the plantation nisei who hated the *luna* is that the sansei in Hawaii are becoming the new *luna*. Nice Japanese girls from Manoa Valley are going through four years of college to get degrees in travel industry management in order to sit behind a small desk in a big hotel, to dole out marching orders to brown-skinned workers, and to take orders from a white man with a bigger desk and a bigger paycheck who never has to complicate his life by dealing with the brown people who make the beds and serve the food.[1] He need only deal with the Nice-Japanese-Girl-ex-Cherry Blossom-Queen, eager to please, who does not know she will never make it to the bigger desk.

The Portuguese *luna* now has the last laugh with this new, unfunny portagee joke: When the portagee was the *luna*, he did not have to pay college tuition to ride that horse. I would like to say to my sister behind the small desk, "Remember where you came from, and take this pledge: We will not be used."

There are a hundred ways to use the racial bourgeoisie. First is the creation of success myths and blame-the-victim ideology. When Asian Americans manage to do well, their success is used against others. Internally, it is used to erase the continuing poverty and social dislocation within Asian-American communities. The

media are full of stories of Asian-American whiz kids.[2] Their successes are used to erase our problems and to disavow any responsibility for them. The dominant culture does not know about
drug abuse in our communities, our high school dropouts, or our
AIDS victims.[3] Suggestions that some segments of the Asian-
American community need special help are greeted with suspi-
cion and disbelief.

External, our successes are used to deny racism and to put
down other groups. African Americans and Latinos and poor
whites are told, "Look at those Asians—anyone can make it in
this country if they really try." The cruelty of telling this to crack
babies, to workers displaced by runaway shops, and to families
waiting in line at homeless shelters is not something I want associated with my genealogy. Yes, my ancestors made it in this
country, but they made it against the odds. In my genealogy, and
probably in yours, are people who went to bed hungry, who lost
land to the tax collector, who worked to exhaustion and ill-
health, who faced pain and relocation with the bitter stoicism
that we call, in Nihongo, *gaman*.[4] Many who came the hard road
of our ancestors did not make it. Their bones are still in the
mountains by the tunnels they blasted for the railroad, still in the
fields where they stooped over the short-handled hoe, and still
in the graveyards of Europe, where they fought for a democracy
that did not include them.

Asian success was success with a dark, painful price. To use
that success to discount the hardship facing poor and working
people in this country today is a sacrilege to the memory of our
ancestors. It is an insult to today's Asian-American immigrants
who work the double-triple shift, who know no leisure, who
crowd two and three families to a home, and who put children

and old folks alike to work at struggling family businesses or doing piecework until midnight. Yes, we take pride in our success,
but we should also remember the cost. The success that is our
pride is not to be given over as a weapon to use against other
struggling communities. I hope we will not be used to blame the
poor for their poverty.

Nor should we be used to deny employment or educational
opportunity to others. A recent exchange of editorials and let-
ters in the Asian-American press reveals confusion over affirmative action.[5] Racist anti-Asian quotas at the universities can give
quotas a bad name in our community. At the same time, quotas
have been the only way we have been able to walk through the
door of persistently discriminatory institutions like the San Francisco Fire Department.[6] We need affirmative action because
there are still employers who see an Asian face and see a person
who is unfit for a leadership position. In every field where we
have attained a measure of success, we are underrepresented in
the real power positions.[7] And yet, we are in danger of being ma-
nipulated into opposing affirmative action by those who say
affirmative action hurts Asian Americans. What is really going
on here? When university administrators have hidden quotas to
keep down Asian admissions, this is because Asians are seen as
destroying the predominantly white character of the university.
Under this mentality, we cannot let in all those Asian over-
achievers and maintain affirmative action for other minority
groups. We cannot do both because that will mean either that
our universities lose their predominantly white character or that
we have to fund more and better universities. To either of those
prospects, I say, why not? and I condemn the voices from my
own community that are translating legitimate anger at ceilings

on Asian admissions into unthinking opposition to affirmative-action floors needed to fight racism.

In a period when rates of educational attainment for minorities and working-class Americans are going down,[8] in a period when America is lagging behind other developed nations in literacy and learning,[9] I hope we will not be used to deny educational opportunities to the disadvantaged and to preserve success for only the privileged.

Another classic way to use the racial bourgeoisie is as America's punching bag. There is a lot of rage in this country, and for good reason. Our economy is in shambles. Persistent unemployment is creating new ghost towns and new soup kitchens from coast to coast. The symptoms of decay—the drugs, the homelessness, and the violence—are everywhere.

From out of this decay comes a rage looking for a scapegoat, and a traditional American scapegoat is the Oriental Menace. From the Workingman's Party that organized white laborers around an anti-Chinese campaign in California in 1877,[10] to the World War II internment fueled by resentment of the success of issei farmers,[11] to the murder of Vincent Chin,[12] and to the terrorizing of Korean merchants in ghetto communities today, there is an unbroken line of poor and working Americans turning their anger and frustration into hatred of Asian Americans. Every time this happens, the real villains—the corporations and politicians who put profits before human needs—are allowed to go about their business free from public scrutiny, and the anger that could go to organizing for positive social change goes instead to Asian bashing.

Will we be used as America's punching bag? We can prevent this by organizing to publicize and to fight racist speech and racist violence wherever we find it. More important, however, Asian Americans must take a prominent role in advocating economic justice. We must show that Asian Americans are allies of the working poor, the unemployed, and the ghetto teenager. If we can show our commitment to ending the economic upheaval that feeds anti-Asian sentiment, the displaced rage that terrorizes Asian Americans will turn on more deserving targets.

If we can show sensitivity to the culture and needs of other people of color when we do business in their communities, we will maintain our welcome there, as we have in the past. I hope we can do this so we can put an end to being used as America's punching bag.

The problem of displaced anger is also an internal problem for Asian Americans. You know the story: the Japanese pick on the Okinawans, the Chinese pick on the Filipinos, and the Samoans pick on the Laotians. On the plantation we scabbed on each other's strikes. In Chinatown, we have competed over space. There are Asian men who batter Asian women and Asian parents who batter their children. There is homophobia in our communities, tied to a deep fear that we are already so marginalized by white society that any additional difference is intolerable. I have heard straight Asian men say they feel so emasculated by white society that they cannot tolerate assertive women or sexually ambiguous men. This is a victim's mentality, the tragic symptom of a community so devoid of self-respect that it brings its anger home.

I love my Asian brothers, but I have lost my patience with malingering homophobia and sexism and especially with using white racism as an excuse to resist change. You know, the "I have to be Bruce Lee because the white man wants me to be Tonto" line. Yes, the J-town boys with their black leather jackets are adorable, but the pathetic need to put down straight women, gays, and lesbians is not. To anyone in our communities who wants to bring anger home, let us say, "Cut it out." We will not be used against each other.

If you know Hawaiian music, you know of the *ha'ina* line that tells of a song about to end. This speech is about to end. It will end by recalling echoes of Asian-American resistance.

In anti-eviction struggles in Chinatowns from coast to coast and in Hawaii, we heard the song *We Shall Not Be Moved*.[13] For the 1990s, I want to say, "We shall not be used." I want to remember the times when Asian Americans stood side by side with African Americans, Latinos, and progressive whites to demand social justice. I want to remember the multiracial ILWU,[14] which ended the plantation system in Hawaii,[15] and the multiracial sugar beet strikes in California that brought together Japanese, Filipino, and Chicano workers to fulfill their dream of a better life.[16] I want to remember the American Committee for the Protection of the Foreign Born, which brought together progressive Okinawans, Koreans, Japanese, Chinese, and European immigrants to fight McCarthyism and the deportation of political activists.[17] I want to remember the San Francisco State College strike[18] and the Asian-American students who stood their ground in multiracial coalition to bring about ethnic studies and lasting changes in American academic life, changes that make it possible for me, as a scholar, to tell the truth as I see it.

In remembering the San Francisco State strike, I also want to remember Dr. Hayakawa and ask what he represented.[19] For a variety of historical and cultural reasons, Asian Americans are particularly susceptible to being used by the dominant society.

Nonetheless, we have resisted being used. We have joined time and again in the struggle for democracy in America. The Asian Law Caucus represents that tradition. The caucus is a concrete manifestation of the pledge to seek a better life for the least advantaged and to work in coalition with other groups. All of you who support the caucus help keep alive a utopian vision of a world free of racism and poverty. You honor the proudest moments in our collective histories.

When I told a friend about this speech, he sent me a news clipping from the *San Francisco Chronicle* about Asian Americans as the retailer's dream.[20] It starts out, "[t]hey're young, [t]hey're single, [t]hey're college-educated, and on the white-collar track. And they like to shop for fun." Does that describe you? Well, it may describe me, too. But I hope there is more to Asian-American identity than that. I hope we will be known to history as a people who remembered the hard road of their ancestors and who shared, therefore, a special commitment to social justice.

This song is now at an end, a song of my hope that we will not be used.

---

1   Dr. Haunani Kay Trask alerted me to the new *luna* phenomenon.

2   See, e.g., David Brand, "The New Whiz Kids: Why Asian-Americans Are Doing so Well, and What It Costs Them," *Time*, 31 August 1987, 42. See generally Al Kamen, "Myth of 'Model Minority' Haunts Asian Americans; Stereotypes Eclipse Diverse Group's Problems," *Washington Post*, 22 June 1992, A1.

3   Cf. Harry H. L. Kitano, *Asian Americans: Emerging Minorities* (Englewood Cliffs, N.J.: Prentice-Hall, 1995) (discussing social problems facing Asian Americans).

4   "Nihongo" is the Japanese word for the Japanese language.

5   For example, individuals such as columnist Arthur Hu have opposed affirmative action admissions programs at colleges, specifically criticizing

race-based admission criteria at the University of California. See Arthur
Hu, "Hu's on First," *Asian Week,* 10 May 1991, 26; 24 May 1991, 12.

6   In 1985, only 35 (2.5 percent) of the 1,380 firefighters in the San Francisco Fire Department were Asian, while Asian men comprised 19.3% of
the male civilian labor force (women were not hired by the SFFD until
1987). *U.S. v. City and County of San Francisco,* 656 F. Supp. 276, 286 n. 10
(1987). A consent decree required hiring Asian Americans. As of August
5, 1990, Asian firefighters still comprised only about 4 percent of the
SFFD. *U.S. v. City and County of San Francisco,* 748 F. Supp. 1416, 1428 n.
10 (1990).

7   According to a 1990 census data and a report by Leadership Education for
Asian Pacifics, Asian Americans are widely dispersed along the economic
spectrum and face discrimination at all levels of employment. Further,
Asian Americans earn less income, per capita, than whites even though
they are often better educated. See generally Elizabeth Llorente, "Asian
Americans Finding Many Doors Closed to Them," *Record (New Jersey),*
23 October 1994, A1. The federal "glass ceiling report" (*Good for Business:
Making Full Use of Human Capital,* [Washington, D.C.: Federal Glass
Ceiling Commission, 1995] stated, "Despite higher levels of formal education than other groups, Asian and Pacific Islander Americans receive a
lower yield in terms of income or promotions."

8   See, e.g., Brenna B. Mahoney, "Children at Risk: The Inequality of
Urban Education," *New York Law School Journal of Human Rights,* 9
(1991):161 (reporting the "declining numbers of urban minority high
school graduates . . . pursuing postsecondary educational opportunities"
and the increasing percentage of poor and minority students performing
below grade level in mathematics and reading).

9   See e.g., Augustus F. Hawkins, "Becoming Preeminent in Education:
America's Greatest Challenge," *Harvard Journal of Law and Public Policy,*
15, (1991):367 (noting that the United States is falling behind other countries in virtually all educational areas, particularly mathematics and the sci-
ences).

10   In the 1870s, white workers, resentful of Chinese laborers (who worked
for lower wages and in worse conditions), pressured politicians into en-
acting a series of anti-Chinese laws that culminated in the Chinese Exclusion Act of 1882.

11   U.S. Commission on Wartime Relocation and Internment of Civilians,
*Personal Justice Denied: Report of the Commission on Wartime Relocation and
Internment of Civilians: Report for the Committee on Interior and Insular Affairs*

(Washington, D.C.: U.S. Government Printing Office, 1982), pp. 42–44. See also Mari J. Matsuda, "Looking to the Bottom: Critical Legal Studies and Reparations," *Harvard Civil Rights–Civil Liberties Law Review,* 22, (1987):363–68 (describing the internment of Japanese Americans during World War II and their subsequent claims for redress).

12   Vincent Chin, a Chinese American, was murdered in Detroit in 1982 by assailants (unemployed auto workers) who thought he was a Japanese person responsible for their loss of jobs. See U.S. Comission on Civil Rights, *Recent Activities against Citizens and Residents of Asian Descent* (1986) pp. 43–44 (giving a brief history of this case).

13   This popular union song based on an old hymn, *I Shall Not Be Moved,* was first sung in 1931 by miners; later versions added newer verses appropriate to the civil rights and anti-war movements. See Tom Glazer, *Songs of Peace, Freedom, and Protest* (New York: D. McKay, 1970), 332–33. For an example of anti-eviction struggle, see e.g. Chester Hartman, "San Francisco International Hotel: Case Study of a Turf Struggle," *Radical America* 12 (June 1978):47–58 (describing activists struggling against the eviction of Chinese-American tenants in San Francisco's Chinatown).

14   The International Longshoremen's and Warehousemen's Union is a progressive, multiracial union active on the West Coast and in Hawaii .

15   See Edward Beechert, *Working in Hawaii: A Labor History* (Honolulu: University of Hawaii Press, 1985); and Sanford Zalburg, *A Spark is Struck: Jack Hall and the ILWU in Hawaii* (Honolulu: University of Hawaii Press, 1979).

16   Thomas Almaguer, "Racial Domination and Class Conflict in Capitalist Agriculture: The Oxnard Sugar Beet Workers' Strike of 1903," *Labor History* 25 (1984):325–50.

17   See Mari Jo Buhle et al., eds., *Encyclopedia of the American Left* (New York: Garland Publishing, 1990), 19–20 (chronicles the general history of the American Committee for Protection of the Foreign Born).

18   See generally Karen Umemoto, "'On Strike!' San Francisco State College Strike, 1968–69: The Role of Asian American Students," *Amerasia* 15 (1989):3–41. (recounting the events at the San Francisco State College strike and Senator Hayakawa's attempt to end it).

19   Ibid., 19.

20   John Berry, "Survey Says Asians Are Dream Customers," *San Francisco Chronicle,* 5 March 1990, C1.

14

Students at Stanford University have sat in, occupied the president's office, gotten arrested, gone on hunger strikes, organized, and protested to get ethnic studies established as a discipline there. This talk on the occasion of Stanford's centennial[1] was part of a concession to students who were demanding that the university address Asian-American issues. One night's presentation was far short of the ethnic studies program Stanford needed, but it was nonetheless an inspiring experience to speak to young activists and to share the stage with two other lecturers, Tamlyn Tomita and George Takei, who are bright stars in the Asian-American constellation.

We speak with pride in Asian-American communities of being like bamboo – bending but never breaking when the typhoons come. Quiet strength, resiliency, and survival are themes that emerge when we tell our family stories and when we tell the collective stories of Asian-American communities. Resilient survival is a major theme in our art – in Asian-American poetry, novels, songs, theater, and film. When we tell our own story, it is infused with the grace and dignity of the bamboo.

A few brave writers and artists are adding to that story, breaking silence about the conflicts and pain in our communities.[2]
Misogyny, alcoholism, abuse, homophobia, greed, ennui,
malaise – a counterstory, not so dignified, not so proud, is also
emerging in our communities, adding to and complexifying our
self-identity as children of the bamboo.

Our efforts at self-description stand in contrast to the way we
are depicted by others. Stereotypes of Asian Americans abound.
We are math nerds. We are gangsters. We are women ready to
serve. We are rich foreigners buying up America. If we wear a
suit and speak without an Asian accent, we can be a television
news reporter, especially if we are young, pretty, and female. But
we are not news makers, unless the news is about those math
nerds or gangsters or rich foreigners buying up America.

My Asian students all have stories of their favorite negative
media image of Asian Americans. They bring me ads encouraging young teens to have eyelid surgery to look more white,
ads encouraging white men to send away for lists of Asian
women anxious to become bride/slaves, ads inviting tourists to
lands where ever-smiling Asians wait to shower guests with luxury.

In addition to media images, there is a vernacular image of
Asians produced by less sophisticated image makers and bigots.
Hate speech directed at Asian Americans is a genre all its own.
There is a list of epithets, jokes about slant-eyes, connotations of
sex and filth, coolie caricatures, and put-downs that circulates in
American popular culture.

During my year of graduate work at Harvard Law School, a
friend and I went to the food services manager to complain about
the paper wrappers they served eggrolls in. The wrappers had a

caricature of a coolie, with a wide, buck-toothed grin and two slanting lines for eyes, hunched over in a subservient posture and wearing an oversized, cone-shaped hat. The manager, a Boston Italian, was surprised by our complaint. "It's how we get the eggrolls from the factory," he said. "No one ever complained before." We told him the picture of the comical, subservient character was racist. "I just don't see it," he said, examining the picture on the limp piece of waxy paper.

He was not the only one who did not see it. Because I did not want to confront food services alone, I carried the wrapper to other Asian students for support. Some thought it was racist; others thought it was merely stupid. Still others said, "Yes, it's racist, but why bother complaining? It's nothing. Let it go."

There have been many times I have let it go. Many times I have sat in dark theaters, there only to seek a little escapist entertainment, only to find myself assaulted by a racist image or epithet thrown in gratuitously without any connection to the plot. In the midst of a stupid, funny movie about Rodney Dangerfield going to college,[3] he remarks about a tape recorder being made by "the j_ps." In a movie about a jazz hero,[4] a song refers to insipid Chinamen. In a satire featuring Marlon Brando and a large lizard,[5] a grinning, subservient Asian character makes repeated, pointless cameo appearances. In each of these instances, I was sitting in a theater enjoying mindless entertainment when I was hit by a racist word or image that was about me. Suddenly the movie stopped for me. I felt attacked, singled out, and degraded. Everyone else in the room went on watching as though nothing assaultive had happened. Following their cue, I, too, remained silent and calmed myself down – "It's just a movie" – and went on with the business of trying to relax on a Saturday night.

"Let it go." We are the bamboo people. We have survived over a hundred years of racist insults on this continent. "It's just words. Let it go." I would like to talk today about why we cannot let it go.

In talking to Asian students and community groups throughout the country, I have come to see that racist images and racist deeds are inseparable. I remember Vincent Chin, Jim Loo,[6] and the five young children murdered in a Stockton schoolyard.[7] Someone hates that grinning, slant-eyed man on the eggroll wrapper enough to kill him. Enough to kill me.

Calling for restriction of racist speech, I have received much criticism from both conservatives and liberals concerned with civil liberties.[8] Many civil libertarians argue that it is not possible to censor racist ideas without violating the First Amendment. From eggroll wrappers to cross burnings, these are expressions of ideas that must be absolutely protected. The solution, they suggest, is to penalize acts, not words. If someone rapes a woman, punish the rapist, not the images that promote violence against women. If someone denies a job to an Asian, punish the racist employer, not the images of Asians as incompetent for certain kinds of work. If someone assaults an Asian, punish the assailant, not the dehumanizing hate speech that makes the assault possible.

According to this formula, a bright line exists between words/images/ideas on the one hand and acts/assaults/discrimination on the other. Looking at the Asian-American experience causes me to question that distinction.

First, because the idea, the word, the image IS an act. A student tells me that she was walking down the street in Westwood when a young teen ran by, calling out a derogatory word for

Chinese American. She described it as an assault. Her response was no different than it would have been if someone had walked up and shoved her. She felt attacked, angry, helpless, fearful, and shocked.

Another student told me of standing in an elevator while two young white lawyers in suits teased an old Asian man whose job it was to deliver the office mail. "So, old man, you have a new mail cart—smart—you're like a real American now." My student, raised to respect the dignity of age, felt humiliated and angry watching the two lawyers treat an elderly gentleman like the office pet.

An Asian-American woman reporter in New York knew it was an assault when a colleague called her a "slant-eyed c_nt" in a professional setting. They were just words, but words stated publicly to remind her of her place and her worth in the eyes of a senior colleague.

In a popular trash movie,[9] an Asian woman is portrayed as getting raped and liking it. Watching this scene, I felt a real and immediate danger, thinking of the thousands of men watching the film and learning that "no" means "yes," that pain and violence are normal, and linking an image of an Asian woman with the message "available for abuse by men."

In all these instances, the words are not merely private expressions of tastes and preferences. They are attacks on the personhood of the target. The recipient perceives them as attacks. "Mere words" is not an accurate description of the function of hate speech and racist imagery.

A second reason that words and acts are inseparable is that acts of discrimination could not happen without an ideological base. Ideology creates violence, and violence creates ideology. Racist words promote racist deeds, and racist deeds promote racist words. Degrading images generate degraded status, and degraded status generates degrading images. In other words, as Marx recognized, the relationship between the ideological and the material world is a dialectic.

If there were no ideology of misogyny, there could be no rape. If there were no ideology of yellow peril, there could have been no internment of Japanese Americans during the war. The idea that one group is subordinate, inferior, untrustworthy, lying, cheating, stealing, and filthy is what makes it possible for gangs of skinheads to attack Asian Americans with baseball bats. The idea that Asian Americans are not really Americans is the reason our history and literature are not considered worthy of study, why our accents and languages are considered threats to the American way. Our opportunities in education, business, and the arts are limited by racist images about what we are good for. Bookkeeper, yes. University professor, no. Gardener, yes. Plant manager, no. Racist ideas, racist images, and racist words limit our life possibilities. Attacking racist acts alone will never get at the underlying ideology that generates the acts in the first place, any more than lopping off the top of a weed will keep it from sprouting again in the next rain.

Finally, the dichotomy between ideology and acts is grounded in a false notion of individual responsibility rather than group responsibility for racism. When we say that the images, the words, and the ideology are less important than the acts of racism, we focus on the search for the few bad guys. The real racists are the ones who come into schoolyards with assault rifles to slaughter Asian schoolchildren. The racist is a rare and terrible bogeymen. He is not us.

This view denies group and collective responsibility for continuing racial subordination, and this denial is why so many people object to affirmative action. It is why they resist any suggestion that the way they presently conduct their lives is racist. If you try to tell a university administrator that it is racist not to have Asians on the faculty, not to have an Asian-American studies department, and not to teach Asian languages, they will object passionately to the charge of racism and offer a whole range of reasons for the status quo—"real" reasons having to do with funds, staffing, and qualifications, not "racist" reasons, because this is not Stockton, and nobody is using an assault gun.

The "find the bad guys" view of racism characterizes the dominant philosophy of the current Supreme Court of the United States. They are dismantling civil rights gains piece by piece, requiring in every instance that victims of discrimination bring to court overt and explicit confessions of racism, the kind of evidence rarely available in the world of corporate, institutionalized exclusion.[10] What the Supreme Court fails to grasp is that racism is not just a few crazy, embittered holdouts engaging in intentional acts of violence or discrimination. Racism is located in all of us, in the images we have absorbed, in the hate words we know, and in the stereotypes about race that are embedded in popular discourse in America. This reality suggests collective responsibility to identify and counter racist ideology.

The image of bamboo bending in the typhoon is a good one to remind us of the survival of Asian Americans. I would like to go beyond that image and ask, What do we need to thrive?

We need a range of images that reflect the variability of our experience and our human condition. Whether the stereotypes are positive—math geniuses and valedictorians—or negative—

inscrutable, sinister villains—they are dehumanizing. Static images deny the fluidity and complexity of actual experience.

We may have to reject positive stereotypes in order to reject negative ones. The image of Asians as cooperative math geniuses may help us get jobs. It may advantage Asians over other minorities in the eyes of the dominant culture. It is evident in the adoption preferences of some white couples who say they do not want a nonwhite baby unless it is an Asian girl. And when that girl grows up, she may benefit from a stereotype that says she is appropriate to report the evening news, especially if she is paired with a silver-haired white man. What is going on here?

A weird form of preference exists for some Asians—assimilated, nonthreatening, and preferably female—in some jobs. This preference comes with a price. When the Asian woman in the newsroom decides to challenge the judgment of her senior colleague, he will be as shocked as if the Xerox machine had chosen to criticize the substance of a memo. The woman who was hired to be good and smart and silent except in scripted appearances is suddenly acting like an equal. Any Asian woman who has been there knows there is a special wrath reserved for those moments. It is disproportionate to the substantive challenge. It is enraged. It is physical. It is scary.

Damned if you do, damned if you don't. Asian women experience backlash when they speak up, but they are also denied opportunities because of fear that they are incapable of speaking up. My Asian law students are asked in interviews whether they can be assertive enough to work as lawyers. They go off to interviews and try to impress hiring partners who have never seen a single media image of an intelligent, assertive, and powerful

Asian-American woman. Words, images, and ideology have real consequences for these students.

We must criticize racist images, and we must demand images that show the full range of Asian-American humanity. I know so many outspoken, activist Asian Americans, but I have never seen an outspoken, activist Asian character on television. I know gay and lesbian Asian Americans, but I have never seen one portrayed in best-selling fiction. I know Asian Americans who are bad in math, who write novels, who sit as federal judges, who teach literature, who hustle in pool halls, and who have rich and complex personalities. I would hate to see this thick collection of humanity live and die with no recording of its presence, with no recognition in the image-making institutions of high and low culture in America.

Asian-American students go out into a world unprepared for their wide range of talents and personalities. I hope they will remain free to invent themselves, even without a store of images to draw from. I hope that they will speak up, act out, lead, and challenge until the world recognizes that an Asian face can mean many things. I hope they will stand tall and unbent when they so choose, even as they remember their ancestors, who survived by bending in the wind.

---

1   Stanford University, May 15, 1990.
2   See, e.g., Asian Women United of California, ed., *Making Waves: An Anthology of Writings by and about Asian American Women* (Boston: Beacon Press, 1989).
3   *Back to School.*
4   *Round Midnight.*
5   *The Freshman.*

6   Vincent Chin, a Chinese American, was beaten to death with a baseball
     bat in 1982 by two unemployed Detroit auto workers who mistook him
     for a person of Japanese descent — the group they blamed for their jobless-
     ness. In 1989, Jim Loo (a Chinese American) was fatally pistol-whipped in
     North Carolina by two white brothers who said they did not like Viet-
     namese people because their relatives had been killed during the Vietnam
     War. Thien Minh Ly, a former UCLA Vietnamese American student
     leader, was stabbed repeatedly and killed in 1996 by a white supremacist
     whose graphic letter to a prison buddy stated, "Oh, I killed a J_p a while
     ago." Thanh Mai died from a fatal head injury in 1993 after being accosted
     by three drunk white males who taunted him with racial slurs such as
     "What the fuck are you looking at g__k?" Yoshihiro Hattori was shot to
     death in 1992 when he went to the wrong door while looking for a Hal-
     loween party. His killer claimed he thought Hattori was a lunatic who
     might hurt him and his family. In 1992, Luyen Phan Nguyen, a University
     of Miami pre-med student, was chased and surrounded by seven white
     males who kicked and beat him to death while yelling racial epithets.

7   At Cleveland Elementary School in Stockton, California, five Asian-
     American students were shot and killed with an assault rifle in January
     1989.

8   See, e.g., Nadine Strossen, "Regulating Racist Speech on Campus: A
     Modest Proposal?" *Duke Law Journal* (June 1990): 484.

9   *Year of the Dragon*.

10   See, e.g., *Washington v. Davis*, 426 U.S. 229 (1976) (holding that racially
     discriminatory results of police qualifying tests were insufficient to estab-
     lish an equal protection violation); *Adarand Constructors, Inc. v. Pena*, 115
     S. Ct. 2097 (1995) (holding that racial classification for purposes of gov-
     ernment affirmative action programs were impermissible absent specific
     proof of de jure discrimination); and *Missouri v. Jenkins*, 115 S. Ct. 2038
     (1995) (holding that racial classifications for purposes of busing were im-
     permissible absent specific proof of de jure discrimination).

15

The Asian American Bar Association of Washington, D.C., and CAPAL[1] invited this fund-raiser address for an event honoring the Asian-American members of Congress.[2] It was an occasion for asking a question critical to the Asian-American community: On what basis do we claim a distinct Asian-American identity?

We are justifiably proud of these honorees. Historically, the Asian-American members of Congress have an above-average voting record in civil rights and human rights. They are consistently pro-family, in the best sense of the word: they vote for better health care, for Headstart, and for human needs. They took leadership positions struggling for the major civil rights legislation of the second reconstruction. They have actively and vigorously supported equality in education, housing, and employment, often using their physical presence as a moral force to contradict the racist arguments of those who opposed the Civil Rights Acts. It is harder to argue that "those people" do not deserve voting rights, fair housing, and nonracist immigration policy when some of "those people" are sitting right there at the table with all the dignified and deserving grace of the nisei World War II veterans.

Many of us feel personally indebted to the Asian-American members of Congress for the doors they opened for us. Someone like Patsy Mink made a whole generation of Asian-American women feel it is possible to speak up and risk controversy. This was a powerful antidote to the other major public image of Asian womanhood that circulated during my youth: Nancy Kwan in high heels singing "I enjoy being a girl" on late-night television. At my law school graduation, an aunt gave me a lei and a hug and said, "We're so proud of you. You're going to be just like Patsy Mink." I realized that in the eyes of a respected relative, "becoming a lawyer" did not mean making a lot of money; it meant "being like Patsy Mink," having the skill and gumption to speak up for the underdog.

This is the ethic our Asian-American members of Congress have exemplified, and this is why it is easy and natural for us to honor them. Given that ease, I would like to complexify our task by asking, Why are we here? Presumably, we feel some connection to these people and their accomplishments. But why are we here? Most of us did not have the opportunity to vote for these honorees. What is the Asian-American identity that makes us claim them as our own? What makes us – Chinese, Pacific Islander, South or Southeast Asian, Korean, Filipino, and Japanese – come together as a group? We are not the same, and we each have unique histories. Why, then, do we gather at fund-raisers like this one to honor a selection of members of Congress who are predominantly – though, thank goodness, not exclusively – Japanese American? Out of what have we created this community we call Asian American?

Our continued political viability depends on a critical under-standing of our identity as an Asian-American coalition. As we de-mand representation in the cabinet of a president we helped elect, we have to answer the identity question. As we demand inclusion in all walks of life — in the academy, in the marketplace, and on the judiciary — we will face the question, sometimes asked in good faith and sometimes asked by those who are threatened by us, Who are Asian Americans? What does a Hmong refugee have in common with a nisei auto mechanic? What are your common in-terests? Who speaks for you? And if many of you are well-off, why should we reserve a place for you in our efforts at inclusion?

Our pan-Asian identity is not a natural, inevitable coalition. It is, like all coalitions, a constructed one. It is nonetheless real and vital.

Saying it is not natural is important because the ideology of racism depends on naturalized notions of racial identity. "Those Asians are just like that." They are naturally greedy, bad drivers, nearsighted, inscrutable, math wizards. Born that way. Can't trust them. Much of our political work as Asian Americans is the task of exploding notions of what is naturally Asian. The work of organizations like MANAA[3] is critically important in chal-lenging the media stereotyping that puts limits on Asian identity.

Our coalition is certainly not natural in the sense of any essence located on the Asian continent. We were not one cul-ture in the places our ancestors came from. In fact, in the land of our ancestors, we were closer to natural enemies with real and often justified enmity and distrust. In my own genealogy, I have Okinawan and Japanese, colonizer and colonized.

Our coalition does not originate in Asia. It is American. It is tied to American history and to the history of colonialism and

militarism. Most of us are living in this country because someone made it impossible for our family to stay in the old country:
the wealthy who drove out the poor, the colonizers who took
the land, the war makers who brought guns and terror, and the
cold warriors who divided nations of kin into parts and parcels.
And when our various families arrived on this continent, they
encountered a uniquely American racism that lumped us all together and planted the seed of an Asian-American coalition, not
a natural coalition but a constructed one.

It was constructed in Chinatown sweatshops, on plantations,
in factories, in fields, and in packing houses where waves of Asian
immigrants who arrived with nothing found themselves living
side by side with those from other Asian-Pacific nations: Korean
camp next to Okinawan camp on a plantation in Hawaii, Filipino pensioner next to Chinese bachelor in a Chinatown hotel,
and Samoan next to Laotian in a crowded housing project. For
over a hundred years and continuing into the present, our immigration patterns and harsh economic circumstances have
brought us together.

Another element critical to our formation as a group was anti-
Asian racism. We may have thought we were all very different
from one another, but the ideology of yellow peril treated us all
the same. Newer Asian groups find they arrive in a country with
over a century of experience in stereotyping and hating Asians.
As the wave of anti-Asian violence that affects our community
continues, we have a stark and physical reminder that being any
kind of Asian is enough to trigger random attacks on the street.
It does no good to flash your student ID or your American Express card to show you are one of those good, hardworking, and
productive Asians. Racism does not work that way. We re-

member Vincent Chin, Jim Loo, and a roll call of Asian-American victims of modern-day lynchings.[4]

These forces – immigration history and racism – were external forces bringing us together. There were also strong internal forces. We chose each other as allies. In multiracial organizations like the ILWU,[5] we banded together to better our circumstances. Asian-American identity reached a high point, many would argue, along with the civil rights and black power movements of the 1960s and 1970s.

I was a child in Los Angeles when Muhammad Ali said, on national television, "Black is beautiful," and mysterious bumper stickers with sleek black panthers began appearing on cars in my neighborhood. This was fascinating, scary, and deeply affecting. Soon, the first cries of yellow power were heard, and working-class Asian gang members started reading political tracts and painting murals of Malcolm X, Ho Chi Min, and Che Guevera on abandoned buildings. Asian college students started sitting in, demanding power within the university, demanding affirmative action for Asians, and linking the bombing in Vietnam and Cambodia to the bombing of Hiroshima: Asian bodies, white supremacy.

This radical pan-Asian nationalism changed the nature of Asian-American politics. The traditional and critically important work of civil rights organizations like the JACL was pushed forward by the nationalist perspective. Some of the lasting contributions of this period of renewed activism and explicit Asian-American coalition building were the establishment of Asian-American studies as a discipline and the victory of the redress movement.[6] As an Asian-American university professor, I know I would not be teaching today if it were not for student activists who forced university administrators to take the talents of Asians in the academy seriously.

So what does the radical politics of yellow power have to do with the fact that we are all sitting together in one room dressed up and eating banquet food? This is one of the paradoxes of life in the 1990s. We may not look like the student radicals of twenty years ago, but their work in solidifying the notion of organizing around Asian-American issues is partly responsible for our being here.

To bring the history of Asian-American identity to the present, changing demographics further complexifies the issue. As the new immigrants rapidly eclipse the old, separate Asian-American identities, such as Korean American or South Asian American, may serve political and cultural purposes more significant for those groups than the pan-Asian identity. New immigrants have special concerns about homeland politics – Korean reunification and Tianamen Square – that raise questions about the goals of traditional Asian-American organizations. Resentment over a disproportionate number of Asian representation slots – on faculties, in Congress, and in Asian-American organizations – going to second-, third-, and fourth-generation Asian Americans rather than newcomers is another reality we have to address in forming our coalition.

Having posited that Asian-American identity is historically constructed by uniquely American circumstances and reinforced by the deliberate practice of pan–Asian-American activism, let me close by suggesting that there is such a thing as an Asian-American issue and an Asian-American position and by suggesting the perhaps disturbing notion that not everyone with an Asian surname is in fact Asian within the meaning of our constructed coalition. To speak plainly, there are some people of Asian descent we might not embrace as representing our community, even if they were elected to Congress. If Asian-American identity is constructed, and constructed in part by a history of activism, then issues do define us.

The Asian-American coalition is defined by the struggle against racism. We support civil rights legislation and organize to stop anti-Asian violence because we see racism and are determined to end it.

We also share an interest in just immigration policy because all of us have immigrant status in our genealogy. At the simple level of self-interest, many of us have family and friends who need to gain U.S. citizenship. On the more complex plane of social justice, we honor those in our family histories who risked life and limb to get here by speaking up for others in similar circumstances, like the Haitian people today. I have been particularly proud that organizations like the JACL, whose members no longer have a direct interest in immigration, have lobbied and fought for justice in immigration law.

Racial equality and fair immigration laws are obvious issues for our coalition. Less obvious issues are continuing sources of tension, a tension that indicates the need for more work, more hard conversation, and more consciousness raising.

What is our position on feminism? On unions? On homelessness? On AIDS? On gays in the military? On the military, period? Some people feel it threatens the coalition to raise issues that are not obviously Asian. I disagree because I believe the key defining element of Asian-American identity is the quest for justice. My ancestors were poor peasants who came to this country because they could not feed their children and pay the taxes in their homeland. My mother grew up barefoot on a sugar plantation. My father was interned at Heart Mountain and volunteered for combat duty in World War II. He is the only one from his machine-gun squad who survived the war. This is my inheritance. It is the only one I will get. In spite of what the dominant culture may believe about rich and privileged Asians, I know that in your family tree there is a history of dignified men and women who sacrificed so you could sit at the banquet table today.

This history is what makes it fair to call any issue of social justice an Asian-American issue, and I believe that is why the Asian-American members of Congress are so easy to honor. They have spoken consistently for the poor, for working people, for small businesses, for immigrant rights, and for women. The ability to make the connection between the injustice we have faced as Asian Americans and the injustice that others face is the ultimate test that marks the line called integrity. I believe our stellar Asian-American delegation has already passed the test, and I believe our Asian-American coalition will live or die by our choice in that regard. May it live long.

---

1 Washington, D.C., February 23, 1993.
2 The Conference on Asian Pacific American Leadership is a group of Asian Pacific American professionals and government employees that works to promote the involvement of Asian Pacific Americans in government service and public policy.
3 The Media Action Network of Asian Americans is a media watchdog group that monitors television programs and movies for portrayals that denigrate and stereotype Asian Americans.
4 Vincent Chin, a Chinese American, was beaten to death with a baseball bat in 1982 by two unemployed Detroit auto workers who mistook him for a person of Japanese descent — the group they blamed for their joblessness. In 1989, Jim Loo (a Chinese American) was fatally pistol-whipped in

North Carolina by two white brothers who said they did not like Vietnamese people because their relatives had been killed during the Vietnam War. Thien Minh Ly, a former UCLA Vietnamese American student leader, was stabbed repeatedly and killed in 1996 by a white supremacist whose graphic letter to a prison buddy stated, "Oh, I killed a J_p a while ago." Thanh Mai died from a fatal head injury in 1993 after being accosted by three drunk white males who taunted him with racial slurs such as "What the fuck are you looking at g__k?" Yoshihiro Hattori was shot to death in 1992 when he went to the wrong door while looking for a Halloween party. His killer claimed he thought Hattori was a lunatic who might hurt him and his family. In 1992, Luyen Phan Nguyen, a University of Miami pre-med student, was chased and surrounded by seven white men who kicked and beat him to death while yelling racial epithets.

5   International Longshoremen's and Warehousemen's Union.
6   Responding to growing public pressure, Congress enacted the Civil Liberties Act of 1988, which authorized the payment of restitution to Japanese Americans and Aleuts interned during World War II (P.L. 100-1383, P.L. 101-162, and P.L. 102-371).

16

SANSEI AND THE LEGACY OF THE NISEI VETS

This lecture was given in my hometown of Honolulu, Hawaii, in July 1992. It was part of a series organized by the Sons and Daughters of the 100th Infantry Battalion. As the children of nisei World War II veterans, the lecture organizers asked, What is our legacy? How do we define it, and what obligations does it produce? For readers unfamiliar with terms of self-reference in the Japanese-American community, nisei is the second generation. The nisei know two cultures intimately: that of their immigrant parents and that of the land they grew up in. Because of the times they lived through, which included the Depression, World War II, and open racism against Japanese Americans, they are heroic figures. The sansei are their children, the third generation, mainly assimilated baby boomers. Sansei are frequently associated in alliteration with the adjective "spoiled." Other terms are defined in the note following this chapter.

It is a very special opportunity to speak before an audience that includes my parents, friends, neighbors, and relatives. This is something I have never done before, and it makes me nervous. Added to this is the responsibility to say something about the nisei vets and their legacy to we sansei. There is no topic as important or as challenging to me. Most of our parents are humble people who will not leave wealth to their children. What they will leave is something more precious than material wealth. It is a history and a set of values, and because this is our primary inheritance, it feels weighty to try to define and understand it.

One part of our cultural heritage I am trying to understand is the ethic of "don't make waves," also memorialized in the saying that warns not to be the *deru kugi*. When I think that this culture was passed on to us by men who fought wars, organized labor unions, took political power away from the Big Five, and generally drank, gambled, and cussed their way through life, I think there is something complex about the warning "Don't make waves." I think it really means "Don't make waves unnecessarily, but raise hell for what you believe is right."

So, what are the obligations of the sansei? First, let me identify the points of consensus. We agree, I think, that our fathers did something special in the World War II effort and that we have a special obligation to preserve the memory of that. We need to collect oral histories, support education and research, and build tangible memorials – monuments, museums, archives, art, and literature – that will recall the nisei vets. Up until now we have assumed that this memory is alive and well. But as we lose the nisei generation, as it becomes clear that we sansei are charged with telling a history we never got right in the first place, we realize we do not know the names, dates, and places – and more important, the range of attitudes and ideas – that constituted the World War II experience. I have never asked my dad if he was scared, for example. And most of what I know about the war I have learned from my mother because she is the talker in the family, and she was not even there. It is time for each family to decide in a systematic way to record the history, and we sansei will have to figure out a way to do this. We should also be present at the museums, universities, legislatures and in Congress to urge institutional support for preserving nisei history.

In addition, we have an obligation to work for the material interest of our parents. We have to support veterans' rights and put pressure on the federal government, when necessary, to avoid deterioration of veterans' benefits and elderly care. We should join and support organizations, like the DAV, that do this.

That's the easy stuff. Now the hard stuff.

First, I think being the child of a vet means we have to ask questions about our relationship to militarism. One thing my father has told me over and over is not to trust someone who claims to be a vet but who never saw combat duty. My dad's vision of war is not a Rambo vision. He lost too many comrades for that. The war he fought in was bloody and hard, and any effort to glamorize war does not honor him or the young nisei boys who left for Europe and never came back. Listen to the stories of marching through freezing rain, soaked to the bone, with no dry place to spend the night. Listen to the stories of taking hills, with the wounded falling and screaming all around, with one hundred killed to move one hundred feet forward. The story I hear is, "War is hell."

When I remember this story, I remember to pause and ask questions before anyone goes to war in my name. Remembrance of the heroism of the 442nd and the 100th should not lapse into easy militarism. Not all wars are the same. Pearl Harbor and Hitler's aggression created a set of historical circumstances that took our fathers to war.

The war the sansei lived through was Vietnam. A different set of historical circumstances. We know now that we were lied to, and that Congress was lied to, about the wisdom of that war. Thousands of American and Vietnamese sons died for that lie. Those who protested were called unpatriotic.

Among those leaders who were bold enough to first call a mistake a mistake were nisei vets like Dan Inouye[1] and Spark Matsunaga,[2] men who knew what war really means. War is hell, and not all wars are the same, and those two facts mean we honor the legacy of our fathers by asking hard questions about militarism, including the militarism that still, to this day, holds much of Hawaii's best land and our economy hostage.

So my first controversial proposal is that the sansei have an obligation to oppose militarism and particularly to oppose any attempt to link our fathers' war against fascism with any unjustified military aggression our government proposes to undertake. If someone asks us to go to war, we should remember the liberators of the 442nd and the 100th, how they were welcomed in little villages all over Europe, and how poor farmers who had barely enough for themselves took food off their tables to give to the nisei soldiers. The nisei soldiers were liberators. They never harmed civilians. Everyone knew why they were there. This has not always been the case with subsequent American military endeavors.

The next obligation the sansei have, I believe, is to oppose racism. It is said sometimes in private and sometimes in public among the nisei vets that their record casualties, the heroic suicide missions, and the horrible combat conditions they faced were connected to the fact that they were Japanese. My father says the words "rear echelon" like he is spitting on the sidewalk.

The plantation boys and working-class *kotonks* were on the front lines, not sitting at desks out of harm's way, and this was a result of racism.

Hawaii, and this nation, has not solved the problem of racial inequality. Two and a half years ago, Los Angeles burned to remind us this is so. On the mainland, my students of Asian descent are reporting increasing acts of violence and racist hate speech directed against them. We tend to think we are immune from this in Hawaii, but as AJAs in Hawaii decline in number and political strength, we must remain vigilant against the glass ceiling and the hidden anti-Japanese attitudes that will keep us out of positions of influence – from corporate boards to seats in the legislature, from university professorships to awards of construction contracts.

I would like to extend my concern about racism, however, beyond the parochial concern over jobs and influence. We have to confront racism because it is stopping us from dealing with our most serious problems, both nationally and locally. Just as racial difference was used to bust early efforts to get better working conditions on the plantations, we have seen how racial difference is used today to destroy our national will to do something about poverty, unemployment, and substandard schools. The Republican Party has succeeded in painting the picture that poverty is a problem of nonwhite people. They use racism to say that crime is caused by Willy Hortons[3] and that inner-city public schools are falling apart because only uneducable black and brown and yellow children go there. Racial stereotypes about "those people" who are naturally lazy and criminal are used to take the focus away from the real causes of poverty and social dislocation: unemployment, corporate crime á la the savings-and-loan scam, a tax system that favors the very rich and breaks the back of the middle class, and the dismantling of the Great Society programs that were making a dent in poverty, illiteracy, and the deterioration of our infrastructure. Racism is used to make poverty and unemployment someone else's problem, to make us turn the other way while our economy collapses all around us.

This has happened in Hawaii as well as the mainland. Large numbers of sansei are now marginally employed, sharing housing with relatives or depending on parents for subsidies to buy homes or send children to college. Many sansei lack secure jobs with decent health care benefits. Others are forced to relocate off island to seek jobs. We have a myth that we Japanese have made it in Hawaii, and we use this myth to distance us from other ethnic groups that are not so well off. The reality is, however, that the economic decline of this nation and this state, the shift from an economy of production to an economy of speculation, has meant a decline in our own economic security. When large numbers of "those people" are poor and unemployed, we are not too far behind. The thriving small businesses of the nisei depended on a broad clientele, including the Filipino, Hawaiian, and immigrant newcomers. Declining buying power in those groups hurts the entrepreneurial efforts of today. This is accompanied by a declining tax base, which means fewer public services.

We do not talk about racism enough in Hawaii and how it is tied to economic decline. As sansei in Hawaii, we must remember the discrimination our parents faced, and we must reject that part of our own heritage that has incorporated racist attitudes. Once it was the Japanese who were thought of as "naturally poor," "untrustworthy," and "criminal." When the Japanese were poor and powerless, they filled the prisons. They went to the gallows in Hawaii when there was a death penalty here. Now other groups are at the bottom, and we sometimes think we are better than they. And yet, it is a paradox of sansei life in these islands that at the same time as there is racism, there is also a positive appreciation of other races. This is the side of my culture I want to preserve.

The memory of an uncle strumming a uke and singing an old song in Hawaiian; the tastes of the rainbow laid out at a family gathering: *lumpia, pipikaula, andagi, kalbi,* and *nishime*; the sound of Nihongo mixed up with Hawaiian and English when the old-timers talk, the way they are sometimes unsure whether a word is Hawaiian or Japanese or English – this wondrous blending of the world's great cultures is part of the miracle of growing up sansei in Hawaii.

This brings me to the third part on my list of sansei obligations: the obligation to preserve the unique set of cultural practices and values that we sometimes refer to as "local." Sometimes when Hawaii Japanese go to school on the mainland, they run into the Asian-American movement, and they are confused because they do not think of themselves as "Asian." They think of themselves as "local." We are both, but our special charge in Hawaii, I think, is to protect and defend the latter.

My father is a *kotonk* who got thrown in with the Hawaii boys and fell in love with them in foxholes and bunkers across France and Italy. They talked pidgin, sang Hawaiian, and lived by a code of honor that included humility, self-sacrifice, and fierce, bull-headed loyalty to the group. The worst sins were to put the self above the group, to show off, to be greedy or pushy, and to act out of individual self-interest. The vets brought home their values and put them in place as public policy as they entered the political arena. They abolished the death penalty in Hawaii, beefed up our public schools, and worked for housing and health care for all. Senator Spark Matsunaga used to say the greatness of a nation is measured in how it takes care of its children and elderly. This ethic of mutual care and concern is the exact opposite of the greedy individualism that has marked public policy in recent years, and we have all suffered from it.

Greedy individualism does not sit well with the Japanese peasant/plantation ethic nor with the *ohana* ethic of our native Hawaiian neighbors. There is a tension between Hawaiians and Japanese that arises from the history of colonialism in these islands that overthrew their government and brought our poverty-stricken ancestors here to work the land the missionaries took. But our common histories make us inevitable allies in the effort to save what is special about Hawaii. The boys of the 442nd and 100th went to war and cried at night when no one was looking because their hearts ached for their beautiful island home.

It is our obligation to preserve that island home, to keep it green and healthy, and to keep the ocean water clear, the reefs alive, and the fish returning with the seasons. The Hawaiian people are our allies in this. We need to confront and overcome past tensions with them and listen to their tale of sovereignty.

I am so proud that the sansei who organized this lecture series have invited the Hawaiians to speak. The Hawaiians have shared with us their precious *aina*, their *ohana* ethnic, their music, their language, and their food. The experience of being local would have no meaning without these gifts. I would like to receive these gifts with respect and listen to what the various Hawaiian groups are saying about our obligations to them. I am not scared of Hawaiian sovereignty.[4] No one is realistically suggesting kicking Japanese out of their homes to make room for Hawaiians. What is suggested is some way to acknowledge that the overthrow of the Hawaiian government was illegal, some way to rectify that wrong.

As the children of liberators, men who defended weaker nations against stronger bullies, we should side with the Hawaiians when they say the armed overthrow of Liliuokalani was outside of American law and ethics. As children of the islands, we should ask how sovereignty can make this a better place. Maybe it will mean opening more land, including the vast acreage held by the military, for construction of homes for homeless Hawaiians. Maybe it will mean more of our federal tax dollars coming home to Hawaii. These things mean jobs, lessening of poverty, and easing of the competition for housing that has led to runaway inflation in the cost of renting or owning homes. Maybe there is something in it for all of us if we treat the Hawaiians fairly.

That is my last controversial proposal: Being sansei in Hawaii means upholding the positive side of local values and standing shoulder to shoulder with native Hawaiians and others who are trying to keep Hawaii a special place. We should support Hawaiian sovereignty and remain in respectful dialogue with Hawaiians.

In conclusion, the invitation to speak here has made me think about who we are and what we have in common. We are sansei. The *issei* are nearly all gone, as hard as that is to believe. Our fathers, who seemed invincible to us and to themselves because they survived the bloodiest battles of the war, are now succumbing to their private wars with the inevitability of aging, as will we in our turn. As the generations unfold, we ask impossible questions like, What is the meaning of being sansei? Our grandparents fought for our right to have food in our mouths. Our parents fought for our right to stand equal and free with all others. We are sansei, and we are the ones who will remember: that war is hell, that racism is wrong, that our families came to this country poor, and that the poor are still our family. We will remember that a group of honorable men survived the war and came home to become our fathers and uncles. They taught us to hold a fishing pole, to strum a uke, to love Hawaii, and to move humbly through life. I hope we will remember their teachings.

---

1   Senator Dan Inouye (D–Hawaii).
2   The late Senator Spark Matsunaga (D–Hawaii).
3   In the presidential campaign of 1988 (in an effort to appeal to white voters), a state GOP committee for George Bush ran incendiary television commercials that featured pictures of Willy Horton, a Black convict who raped a woman while on furlough from prison.

A Note on Terminology
and Social History

The preceding speech is reprinted as given, in an effort to keep the Hawaii audience at the center. Rather than interrupting the text with footnotes, a glossary is provided below for readers unfamiliar with local Hawaii usage.

In addition, a brief social history is useful. The Japanese were brought to Hawaii at the turn of the century to work on the sugar plantations. Their story of immigrant ascendency, starting with nothing and rising to the middle class, is a noble one from their own perspective and a problematic one for Native Hawaiians. The Hawaiians lived in relative comfort in Hawaii for thousands of years before the Euro/American invasion that decimated their population and confiscated their lands. An illegal, U.S.-backed coup resulted in the destruction of the sovereignty of the Native Hawaiian government.

From the Hawaiian perspective, the coming of impoverished immigrants to work on the sugar plantations consolidated the economic, spatial, and social degradation of the Hawaiians. Tension between immigrants and Natives was exacerbated by an economic elite that deliberately planned to pit one nonwhite group against another. Nonetheless, as discernable local culture has emerged among nonwhites in Hawaii, and a love of Hawaiian culture, music, food, dance, and—most important—ethos is a real part of local Japanese culture. The Hawaiian ethic of generosity, group identity, love of the land, and anti-individualism is something widely admired and valued by many non-Hawaiians of Asian descent.

This complex relationship between Hawaiian and Japanese in Hawaii is alluded to in the text above.

TERMINOLOGY

deru kugi (p. 182) Literally, "sticking out nail," from the well-known expression in Japanese that says, more or less, "The nail that sticks out gets clobbered." The meaning is the opposite of the American expression "The squeaky wheel gets the grease."

The Big Five (p. 182) The interlocking sugar/shipping companies that dominated political and economic life in Hawaii before the war.

DAV (p. 183) The Disabled American Veterans organization. Nearly all the Nisei vets were wounded in combat, earning the 100th the honorific nickname "the purple heart battalion."

kotonks (p. 184) Japanese Americans born on the mainland United States whose heads were said to make a "kotonk" sound when they hit the ground in brawls during their first encounters with the Hawaii boys.

lumpia (Filipino eggrolls), *pipikaula* (Hawaiian cured beef), *andagi* (Okinawan donuts), *kalbi* (Korean barbecue ribs) and *nishime* (Japanise pickled vegetables) are all typical local party fare.

AJAs (p. 185) Americans of Japanese Ancestry.

Nihongo The Japanese word for the Japanese language.

pidgin A language that sociolinguists call "Hawaiian Creole" and that developed as a result of interethnic contact on the plantation and subsequent residential, social, and educational segregation of pidgin speakers. Most Nisei in Hawaii are bilingual speakers of Hawaiian Creole English and Japanese. Most speak standard English as well.

ohana ethic (p. 185) This refers to the Hawaiian concept of *ohana,* or extended family.

'āina (p. 188) The Hawaiian word for land, but encompassing more than the physical, Western notion of land. In the Hawaiian cosmology, the people are genealogically related to the land and to the natural world, and the land is a living thing.

sovereignty (p. 189) Refers to the movement among Hawaiians to reclaim their legal status as a nation, just as American Indians have limited sovereignty and self-governance rights. The sovereignty movement encompasses claims for return of Hawaiian lands and reparation for the losses Hawaiians have suffered.

Lili 'uokalani (p. 189) The last queen of Hawaii, imprisoned and overthrown by Americans in 1893.

issei (p.189) The first generation of immigrants to Hawaii, who began arriving over one hundred years ago.

Epilogue and Acknowledgments

On a sunny day in April some years ago, thousands gathered for a march on Washington supporting gay rights. I was struck by the many college contingents, so young, so beautiful, so hip in the way of the marginalized – gathering up power and self-worth from what the dominant culture rejects: thrift-market clothes, startling hair, and *attitude*. "We're here, we're queer, we're fabulous, get used to it," they chanted. Black, white, yellow, brown, arm and arm, an army of laughter and love. I thought of how rare it is in our divided nation to see young people of different races in lively, loving, public social interaction. I thought, "Affirmative action did this. The university is the place where these young people, different as they are, can learn to engage in politics together."

As this book goes to press, the backlash against gay rights, racial justice, and feminism continues. Judges and politicians are dismantling the affirmative action programs that gave people like me the chance to become a university professor, that give young college students the chance to learn how to work in coalition. As I hear, again and again, the message, "You don't belong here," I am continually grateful to those who help me know that message for what it really is: the last gasp of the old order. In the ten-year span that the speeches and papers in this book traversed, I have seen generations of students smarter, more diverse, more challenged, and more challenging in their pursuit of knowledge than any who have ever inhabited the academy. Their many-hued faces are beautiful, filling and making new spaces in which men and women, gay and straight, all races, all religions, can learn and laugh together. In spite of the backlash, they have shown us the possibility of living with an open heart toward difference. The audience I imagined for this book was those students.

My gratitude toward students — those who struggled through my classes, those who came to my presentations, those who march in the streets — is profound. I owe a specific debt to those who worked as my research assistants in the years I was on the road giving these speeches: Lila Gardner, Lily Hsu, Lisa Lim, Clarel Cyriaque, Danny Wan, Kiya Kato, Ramona Ortiz, and Haydeh Behbehani. Jennifer Bosco and Elliot Hinds were the ones who found my old speeches and papers scattered in file cabinets and who found the charming and talented Ms. Deb Chasman at Beacon Press to make them a book. Gi Hyun An, Chan Park and Susan Epps read and edited the entire manuscript. Liane Nomura and Kristen Shigemura provided additional proofreading.

Deans, faculty, librarians, and staff of four law schools supported this work: the University of Hawaii William S. Richardson School of Law, the Stanford Law School, the UCLA School of Law, and the Georgetown University Law Center. Dean Judy Areen at Georgetown and Associate Dean Mark Tushnet provided research support at the particularly critical stage of editing and rewriting these chapters. Ms. Jennifer Fairfax was both skilled and patient in preparing the manuscript. Zick Rubin of the Palmer and Dodge firm provided me with excellent legal advice regarding publishing a book.

In all I do, I am sustained by my families. My political family is critical race theory, that band of law professors to whom I owe thanks for my theoretical grounding.

My found family is the Lawrences, who welcomed me and celebrated my work since I first walked into their homestead. To Dr. Margaret Lawrence, my sisters Sara Lawrence Lightfoot and Paula Wehmiller, and their tribes, many thanks.

The Matsuda family—Don, Kimi, Bill, Jimbo, Tracy Langhurst, Ben, and Lucas—gives me more love than one person could use in one lifetime, leaving a great surplus to draw on in those moments in my professional life that are less than loving. The Matsuda clan's hands-on sharing of childrearing has created a cradle of security from which my children will walk away loved and happy. There is nothing that means more to me.

Finally, this book is dedicated to Charles Lawrence. Those who know his work will feel its influence on every page of this book. Like his father, he is a passionate defender of freedom who counsels truth in all things. His presence at the back of the room when I first spoke many of the words that make up this volume required that I tell the truth as best I could. For love and politics, for shared struggle in life's most difficult work—parenting—and for the stories I will never tire of, my heart to Charles.

And, as it will always be, love to Maia, Kimi, and Paul.

Index